get crocked.

Slow Cooker
5 Ingredient
Favorites

Contents

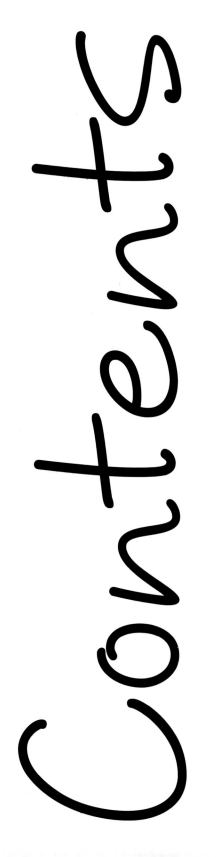

93

138

134

209

Beef Nachos 76

As a busy wife and mother, I know firsthand that it can be difficult to fit cooking for the family into your schedule, but, personally, there are few things I value more than spending time around the table with my loved ones. Plus, eating out can get expensive! That's why I love simple slow cooker recipes. I've compiled my favorites in this book so that busy families like mine don't have to sacrifice delicious meals or one another's company. How easy are we talking? Barring salt, pepper and optional add-ins, you can count the ingredients for each recipe on one hand. A few minutes of prep followed by a few hours in the slow cooker, and dinner (or breakfast, or dessert) is done! I hope that these simple, 5-ingredient recipes help you create time to enjoy home-cooked meals and precious moments with your nearest and dearest.

Happy Crocking!

xOxO, Jenn Bare

Slow Cooker 101

The only thing easier than whipping up a 5-ingredient recipe is using your slow cooker to do so. That being said, these five super-smart tips will take your quick, simple meal up a notch—so you'll have a truly great dinner (or breakfast, or dessert) to put on the table with hardly any effort. Shh...I won't tell.

1. Size Things Up

Make sure your slow cooker is the appropriate size. A family of two to three should use a 4-quart slow cooker for regular meals and a 6-quart slow cooker for big pots of soup or stew. A model that's too big can cause food to cook too quickly or burn. For best results, make sure your slow cooker is ½ to ⅔ of the way full. Underfilling the slow cooker can dry out your meal.

2. Layer It In

Sure, you can just toss all your ingredients into the slow cooker—but placing them in a certain order often makes for better texture in the final product. Root vegetables, such as carrots and potatoes, take longer to cook than meat, for instance, so you should place them on the bottom of the slow cooker. And while you're at it, chop ingredients in a uniform size; it's another step that helps ensure everything cooks evenly.

3. Time It Right

Use a programmable slow cooker to let meals cook all day while you're gone. It will automatically switch to WARM when the timer goes off. Keep in mind that you want to save some ingredients for last, though. Dairy products, such as sour cream and cream cheese, can break down if left cooking for hours, so add them during the last 15 to 30 minutes of cooking (unless otherwise specified). The same rules apply when it comes to breakfast. If your recipe calls for eggs, dairy or meat (ingredients that can be overcooked), prep the meal in a slow cooker liner or large bowl before you go to sleep, then set your alarm according to the cook time. When you wake up, all you'll have to do is add the liner to the slow cooker and turn it on before you go back to bed for a few more hours. Another food that's easy to overcook: pasta. Only add noodles during the last hour of cooking to keep them from turning to mush. You can also precook pasta until it's al dente and add it to the slow cooker during the last 15 minutes of cooking.

4. Practice Your Patience

Resist the urge to take a peek while your food's still simmering. If you lift the lid, moisture and heat can escape, causing the dish to dry out and take longer to cook. So always keep the lid on your slow cooker when it's in use (unless otherwise specified).

5. Add Finishing Touches

If you want to make your meal even more mouth-watering, stick it in the oven to brown up a bit before serving. Many slow cooker inserts, but not lids, are oven-safe. (Word to the wise: Make sure you use potholders—the stoneware will be hot!)

Up & At 'Em

Mornings shouldn't be more difficult than they have to be. With these recipes, they're a snap!

Cinnamon Rolls

YIELD 10 rolls **I COOK TIME** 3 to 4 hours

Ingredients

½ c. butter, softened

1 T. ground cinnamon

1 c. packed brown sugar

1 (1-lb.) loaf frozen bread dough, thawed

¼ c. heavy cream, plus more for optional glaze

½ c. powdered sugar, optional

Directions

1. In a small bowl, combine butter, cinnamon and brown sugar.

2. Roll thawed dough out into a 12- by 6-in. rectangle. Top with cinnamon-sugar mixture. Roll dough into a tight log. Moisten edges slightly and seal shut. Slice into 10 pieces and arrange rolls in greased slow cooker.

3. Cover slow cooker with a dish towel and let rolls sit for 30 minutes to 1 hour, or until rolls have doubled in size. Add heavy cream.

4. Cover and cook on LOW for 3 to 4 hours, or until the rolls are cooked through.

5. If desired, mix 3 T. heavy cream with powdered sugar to create a glaze. Drizzle over cinnamon rolls and serve.

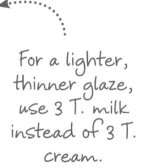

For a lighter, thinner glaze, use 3 T. milk instead of 3 T. cream.

Apple Butter

YIELD 8 cups **I** **COOK TIME** 11 to 13 hours

Ingredients

15 medium apples, peeled, cored and finely chopped

¼ c. honey

3 T. ground cinnamon

½ t. ground cloves

½ t. ground nutmeg

Directions

1. Place apples in slow cooker.

2. In a medium bowl, combine the remaining ingredients. Pour mixture over apples. Do not stir.

3. Cover and cook on LOW for 8 hours, mashing apples and stirring ingredients at the 6 hour mark.

4. After the mixture finishes cooking, remove and transfer to a food processor. Process until butter is smooth. Cool in jars and store in the refrigerator.

Any kind of apples will do in this recipe, so I use a combination.

Cranberry Maple Syrup

YIELD 10 portions **I** **COOK TIME** 3 to 4 hours

Ingredients

¾ c. pure maple syrup

1 c. cranberries

1 T. unsalted butter

1 T. orange zest

Directions

1. Add maple syrup and cranberries to slow cooker.

2. Cover and cook on HIGH for 2 to 3 hours, or until the mixture begins to bubble and cranberries begin to pop.

3. Reduce heat to LOW.

4. Mash berries until smooth, cover and cook on LOW for 1 hour.

5. Stir in butter and orange zest, then serve.

For a fancy presentation, you can stir in whole fresh cranberries before serving.

Fruit Crumble
Breakfast Cobbler

YIELD 4 portions **I COOK TIME** 7 to 9 hours

Ingredients

8 medium apples, peeled, cored and sliced

¼ c. honey

2 t. ground cinnamon

2 T. butter, melted

4 c. granola

Directions

1. Add all ingredients (except 2 c. of granola) to slow cooker and stir. Top with remaining granola.

2. Cover and cook on LOW for 7 to 9 hours.

Granola Guidelines

Make granola at home with ½ cup oil, ½ cup honey, 4 c. oats and 2 c. chopped nuts. Heat oil and honey in an oven-proof pan over low until bubbling. Combine with oats and nuts and bake at 350 degrees F for 30 minutes, stirring three times.

Spiced
Applesauce

YIELD 4 portions **I**
COOK TIME 6 hours 30 minutes
to 8 hours 30 minutes

Ingredients

8   medium apples, peeled, cored
and thinly sliced

½ c. water

½-¾ c. packed brown sugar

½ t. pumpkin pie spice

Directions

1. Combine apples and water in
slow cooker.

2. Cover and cook on LOW for 6 to
8 hours.

3. Stir in brown sugar and
pumpkin pie spice.

4. Cook on LOW for another 30
minutes, stir and serve.

Cream of Wheat

YIELD 4 portions **I COOK TIME** 7 to 8 hours

Ingredients

⅔ c. cream of wheat

3 ¾ c. water

½ t. salt

1 T. pure maple syrup or brown
   sugar, to taste

Directions

1. Combine all ingredients in slow cooker.

2. Cover and cook on LOW for 7 to 8 hours.

Hit healthy food groups at the start of your day by topping with bananas or strawberries.

Lemon-Glazed
Blueberry Pancakes

YIELD 4 portions **I COOK TIME** 1 hour

Ingredients

1   c. Bisquick

½   c. milk, plus more to garnish

1   egg

½   c. blueberries

1 ½   t. lemon juice, to garnish

½   c. powdered sugar, to garnish

Directions

1. Cut a piece of parchment paper to fit the bottom of slow cooker. Insert the paper and grease, along with sides of slow cooker.

2. Mix Bisquick, milk and egg until well combined. Pour ½ the batter in slow cooker. Add blueberries and top with remaining batter.

3. Cover and cook on HIGH for 1 hour, or until a toothpick inserted into the center comes out clean.

4. Loosen edges of the pancake with a butter knife and flip slow cooker to remove.

5. If desired, whisk lemon juice, 1 ½ t. milk and powdered sugar together in a small bowl. Drizzle over pancake, cut and serve.

If you prefer, forget the glaze and garnish with powdered sugar and blueberries.

Blueberry Butter

YIELD 5 cups **I COOK TIME** 6 hours

Ingredients

- 8 c. blueberries, pureed
- 2 c. sugar
- 1 lemon, zested and juiced
- 2 t. ground cinnamon
- ½ t. ground nutmeg

Directions

1. Add blueberries to slow cooker.

2. Cover and cook on LOW for 1 hour, stirring once when finished.

3. Crack lid slightly so steam can escape. Continue to cook on LOW for 3 hours.

4. When 1 hour remains, add sugar, lemon zest, lemon juice, cinnamon and nutmeg. Remove lid and cook on HIGH for 1 hour, stirring mixture every 10 minutes to prevent burning.

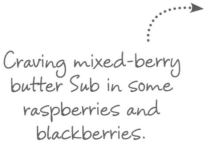

Craving mixed-berry butter Sub in some raspberries and blackberries.

Strawberry Lemonade Oatmeal

YIELD 2 to 3 portions **I COOK TIME** 7 to 9 hours

Ingredients

¾ c. old-fashioned oats

1 ½ c. water

½ c. strawberries, chopped

½–1 t. pure lemon extract

1–2 T. agave nectar

½–1 t. lemon zest, optional

Directions

1. Combine everything (except agave and lemon zest) in greased slow cooker.

2. Cover and cook on LOW for 7 to 9 hours.

3. Stir well until oatmeal reaches a uniform consistency, mashing berries as you mix.

4. Stir in agave and lemon zest, if using, and serve.

Serve with a side of apple butter slathered on whole wheat toast for a healthy, hearty a.m. treat.

Strawberry Jam

YIELD 6 to 8 cups **I COOK TIME** 10 to 11 hours

Ingredients

4 (16-oz.) packages strawberries, stems removed and quartered

3 c. sugar

1–2 (3 ½-oz.) boxes pectin powder

Directions

1. Place strawberries in slow cooker. Mash to create liquid. Add sugar and 1 box pectin. Mash mixture until well combined.

2. Cover and cook on LOW for 10 hours, stirring occasionally.

3. If your berries have not gelled, add more pectin, cover and cook on HIGH for 1 hour.

4. Store finished product in hot canning jars or sealable containers and refrigerate.

⟫ Can I Eat It Yet?

To see if your jam is ready, place a spoonful onto an ice-cold plate and let it sit for 1 to 2 minutes. Touch the jam to assess whether it is setting. If the jam is still runny and saucy, add more pectin and cook until it changes form.

Creamy
Old-Time
Oatmeal

YIELD 6 to 8 portions **|**
COOK TIME 6 hours

Ingredients

1 ⅓   c. old-fashioned oats

2 ½   c. plus 1 T. water

   1   dash salt

Directions

1. Mix the oats, water and salt in slow cooker.

2. Cover and cook on LOW for 6 hours, or until creamy.

Crème Brûlèe French Toast

YIELD 4 to 6 portions **I COOK TIME** 7 to 8 hours

I garnish with powdered sugar and caramel syrup.

Ingredients

12 oz. challah or sweet bread, cut into chunks

4 c. milk

½ c. brown sugar

3 eggs

1 t. pure vanilla extract

¼ t. salt, optional

Prepared caramel sauce, warmed, optional

Directions

1. Insert a plastic slow cooker liner into a medium bowl. Add bread.

2. In a mixing bowl, combine milk, brown sugar, eggs, vanilla and salt. Pour mixture over bread cubes and press bread lightly with back of a large spoon to moisten completely.

3. Cover and refrigerate for 4 to 24 hours. Remove liner and transfer to slow cooker.

4. Cover and cook on low for 7 to 8 hours, or until a knife inserted in the center comes out clean.

5. Turn off slow cooker and let stand for 30 minutes. Carefully lift plastic liner and transfer French toast to a cutting board.

6. Slice French toast or spoon into serving dishes.

Sausage Gravy

YIELD 5 portions **I COOK TIME** 7 to 8 hours

Ingredients

- 1 lb. pork sausage
- ¼ c. butter
- ¼ c. all-purpose flour
- ¼ t. pepper
- 2 ½ c. milk
- 2 (10 ¾-oz.) cans cheddar cheese soup
- 10 biscuits, to serve

Directions

1. Brown sausage in a skillet over medium heat. Drain and remove.

2. Add butter to the skillet and melt. Stir in flour and pepper until smooth. Gradually whisk in milk and soup. Bring to a boil. Cook and stir for 2 more minutes, or until thick and bubbly. Stir in sausage.

3. Transfer mixture to slow cooker.

4. Cover and cook on LOW for 7 to 8 hours.

5. Spoon over biscuits and serve.

Use whole milk or cream to make this gravy stick-to-your-ribs thick.

Creamy, Dreamy
Grits

YIELD 4 portions **I COOK TIME** 8 hours 15 minutes to 9 hours 15 minutes

Stir in milk or cream, a little at a time, to thin grits.

Ingredients

1 ½ c. grits

7 c. water

2 T. butter

½ T. salt

½ t. pepper

1 (8-oz.) container mascarpone cheese

Directions

1. Add all ingredients (except the cheese) to greased slow cooker. Stir to combine.

2. Cover and cook on LOW for 1 hour. Reduce heat to WARM, cover and cook for 7 to 8 hours.

3. Stir grits and fold in cheese.

4. Cover and cook on LOW for 15 minutes.

5. Reduce heat to WARM and serve.

Simple
Breakfast
Casserole

YIELD 6 to 8 portions **|**
COOK TIME 6 to 7 hours

Ingredients

1   lb. sausage

1   (32-oz.) bag frozen shredded
    hashbrowns

3   c. shredded sharp cheddar
    cheese

12 eggs, beaten

¼   c. milk

    Salt, to taste

    Pepper, to taste

Directions

1. Brown sausage in a skillet over medium heat. Drain and remove.

2. Place 1/3 of the hash browns in the bottom of a slow cooker, followed by 1/3 of the cheese and 1/3 of the sausage. Repeat layers until hash browns, cheese and sausage are gone.

3. Whisk eggs and milk together in a bowl. Pour the mixture in slow cooker. Add salt and pepper to taste.

4. Cover cook on LOW for 6 to 7 hours.

If you want, you can use 2 cartons of egg substitute in place of eggs and milk.

Ham and Hash Brown Egg Bake

YIELD 8 portions **I COOK TIME** 6 to 8 hours

Ingredients

1   lb. ham

1   (32-oz.) package frozen hash browns

2   c. shredded cheese

18 eggs

1   c. milk

   Salt, to taste

   Pepper, to taste

Directions

1. Add ½ the ham, ½ the hash browns and ½ the cheese to slow cooker. Repeat until ingredients are gone.

2. In a separate bowl, combine eggs, milk, salt and pepper. Pour mixture into slow cooker.

3. Cover and cook on LOW for 6 to 8 hours.

⫸ Budget Breakfast

If you want to feed a crowd on a dime, egg-based dishes are the way to go. I love this recipe because it's inexpensive to make but keeps my diners full well past lunchtime. If you've got an active day ahead, I suggest you do the same!

Puff Pancake

YIELD 6 portions **I COOK TIME** 1 hour

Ingredients

1 c. all-purpose flour

½ t. salt

6 eggs

1 c. milk

3 T. unsalted butter, melted

Powdered sugar, to garnish

Fruit of your choice, to garnish

Directions

1. Combine flour and salt in a bowl. Create a small well in the middle of the dry ingredients.

2. In a separate small bowl, whisk together eggs, milk and melted butter. Pour ½ of the milk-egg mixture in the well you formed in the dry ingredients. Mix ingredients. Once combined, add remaining milk-egg mixture, and stir until combined. Do not over mix. Pour batter into greased slow cooker.

3. Cover and cook on HIGH for 1 hour, or until the pancake has "puffed." Cool slightly before serving with powdered sugar and fresh fruit.

Allowing your eggs and milk to reach room temperature before adding them will yield the best results.

Party Pleasers

Take the heavy lifting out of hosting with these simple recipes—they were made for easy entertaining!

Baked Cherry Brie

YIELD 4 portions **I** **COOK TIME** 1 to 2 hours

Ingredients

1   (8-oz.) round Brie

⅓ c. dried cherries, chopped

1   T. packed brown sugar

1   T. water

½ t. balsamic vinegar

¼ c. toasted almond slivers, optional

Directions

1. Place Brie in slow cooker. Combine remaining ingredients (except almonds) in a small bowl and pour over Brie. Top with almonds, if desired.

2. Cover and cook on HIGH for 1 to 2 hours.

⟩ Tip-Top Toppings

Sometimes, I switch things up and serve this recipe topped with an apple almond mixture. Combine ½ c. chopped apples, ¼ c. chopped almonds and ¼ t. cinnamon in a small bowl, then sprinkle on top of the cooked Brie.

Mulled Cider

YIELD 8 to 10 portions |
COOK TIME 3 hours

Ingredients

- 8 cups apple cider
- ½ c. frozen orange juice concentrate
- ½ c. packed brown sugar
- ½ t. whole allspice
- 1 ½ t. whole cloves
- 1 apple, sliced, optional
- 8 cinnamon sticks, to garnish

Directions

1. Tie all whole spices in cheesecloth bag, then combine all ingredients in slow cooker.

2. Cover and cook on LOW for 3 hours.

3. Serve in individual mugs and garnish with cinnamon sticks.

Garlic Dip

YIELD 8 portions | **COOK TIME** 1 or 2 hours

This stuff is addictive! For a slightly lighter alternative, substitute mayonnaise with plain Greek yogurt.

Ingredients

- 2 (8-oz.) packages cream cheese, cubed
- ⅔ c. mayonnaise
- 2 bulbs garlic, peeled, diced and smashed

Directions

1. Add cream cheese to slow cooker set to HIGH. Top with mayonnaise and stir until mixture is smooth. Add garlic and stir.

2. Cover and cook on HIGH for 1 hour or on LOW for 2 hours.

Creamy Tomato Dip

YIELD 15 to 20 portions | **COOK TIME** 1 to 2 hours

Ingredients

- 1 ½ (8-oz.) packages cream cheese
- 1 (12-oz.) can Rotel, drained
- 1 lb. ground sausage
- 2 large jalapeño peppers

Directions

1. Combine cream cheese and Rotel in slow cooker.

2. Brown sausage in a skillet over medium heat. Drain, transfer to slow cooker and stir.

3. Cover and cook on LOW for 1 to 2 hours, or until heated through, stirring frequently.

4. Garnish with jalapeños and serve.

Spread this dip onto your grilled cheese for a delish grown-up take on the childhood classic.

Beer Cheese Dip

YIELD 8 portions **I** **COOK TIME** 30 to 40 minutes

Make this recipe even more mouthwatering by adding a packet of ranch dressing mix.

Ingredients

½ c. beer

¼ t. hot sauce

1 lb. Velveeta cheese, cubed

1 t. dry mustard

1 t. Worcestershire sauce

Directions

1. Mix all ingredients in slow cooker.

2. Cover and cook on HIGH for 30 to 40 minutes, or until cheese melts.

3. Stir mixture, reduce heat to LOW and serve.

Apple Brandy

YIELD 8 portions **|**
COOK TIME 3 to 4 hours

Ingredients

- 1 (750-ml) bottle apple-flavored wine
- 2 c. apple cider
- 1 c. peach brandy
- 1 cinnamon stick

Directions

1. Combine all ingredients in slow cooker.

2. Cover and cook on LOW for 3 to 4 hours.

Serve brandy warm, cold or at room temperature.

Bacon-Stuffed Mushrooms

YIELD 10 portions **I** **COOK TIME** 1 hour 30 minutes to 2 hours

Ingredients

- 1 (14-oz.) package medium-sized mushrooms
- Salt, to taste
- Pepper, to taste
- 1 c. shredded Monterey Jack cheese
- ¼ c. plus 2 T. bread crumbs
- 1 egg white
- 6 bacon slices
- 1 t. Worcestershire sauce, optional
- 1 t. garlic powder, optional

Directions

1. Remove mushroom stems and set aside. Place mushroom caps in slow cooker, hollow side up, and sprinkle with salt and pepper.

2. Mince mushroom stems and transfer to a medium bowl. Add remaining ingredients and stir.

3. Transfer mixture into mushroom caps and press to stuff.

4. Cover and cook on HIGH for 1 hour 30 minutes to 2 hours.

Garnish with parsley to instantly class up your presentation.

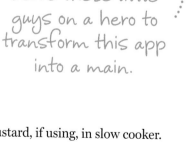

BBQ Meatballs

YIELD 12 to 15 portions **I** **COOK TIME** 6 to 10 hours

Serve these little guys on a hero to transform this app into a main.

Ingredients

1 ½ c. chili sauce

1 c. grape or apple jelly

3 t. brown spicy mustard, optional

1 lb. ground beef

1 egg

3 T. dry bread crumbs

½ t. salt

Directions

1. Combine chili sauce, jelly and spicy mustard, if using, in slow cooker. Mix well.

2. Cover and cook on HIGH while preparing meatballs.

3. Mix together remaining ingredients and shape into 30 balls. Bake at 400 degrees F for 15 to 20 minutes. Drain well. Transfer meatballs to slow cooker and stir to coat.

4. Cover and cook on LOW for 6 to 10 hours.

Homemade
Salsa

YIELD 10 portions **I COOK TIME** 3 hours

Ingredients

12 Roma tomatoes, cored and chopped

4 cloves garlic, minced

1 medium yellow onion, diced

2 jalapeños, chopped and stems removed

¼ c. cilantro leaves

Salt, to taste

Pepper, to taste

Directions

1. Combine the tomatoes, garlic, onions and jalapeños in slow cooker.

2. Cover and cook on HIGH for 3 hours, or until vegetables are soft.

3. Let mixture cool. If you like a thinner salsa, transfer to a blender, cover and process until salsa reaches a desirable texture.

4. Stir cilantro, salt and pepper into salsa, if desired, and serve.

For milder salsa, seed jalapeños before adding them to the slow cooker.

Cocktail Weenies

YIELD 8 to 10 portions **I COOK TIME** 3 to 4 hours

Try this holiday twist: Sub cranberry jelly for grape jam.

Ingredients

1   (16-oz.) package little smokies

1   small yellow onion, diced

1   c. chili sauce

¾   c. grape jam

2   t. Dijon mustard

Directions

1. Combine all ingredients in slow cooker and stir well until well combined.

2. Cover and cook on LOW for 3 to 4 hours, stirring occasionally.

Buffalo Cheesy Chicken Dip

YIELD 8 to 10 portions **I** **COOK TIME** 1 hour

Ingredients

1   (8-oz.) package cream cheese, softened

½ c. blue cheese or ranch dressing

½ c. blue cheese crumbles

½ c. buffalo sauce, plus more for a spicier taste

1   rotisserie chicken, shredded

1   stalk celery, chopped, optional

Tortilla chips, to serve

Directions

1. Combine cream cheese, dressing, blue cheese and buffalo sauce in slow cooker. Stir in chicken.

2. Cover and cook on LOW for 1 hour, or until cheese is melted and dip is heated throughout.

3. Stir in celery, if desired, and serve dip with tortilla chips.

Crave more heat? Add a few diced chili peppers and a couple dashes of hot sauce.

Pineapple Pepper
BBQ Meatballs

YIELD 8 portions **I COOK TIME** 2 hours 30 minutes to 3 hours

Ingredients

1 (32-oz.) package frozen meatballs, thawed

1 (20-oz.) can pineapple chunks, drained

2 bell peppers, cut into bite-sized pieces

1 (18-oz.) bottle BBQ sauce

Directions

1. Add meatballs, pineapple and peppers to slow cooker. Pour BBQ sauce over ingredients and stir.

2. Cover and cook on HIGH for 2 hours 30 minutes to 3 hours, stirring occasionally.

⫸ Sweet, Sour Twist

This recipe works as a base for another one of my favorites: Tangy Sweet and Sour Meatballs. Just add 3 T. vinegar, 1 T. soy sauce and ½ c. packed brown sugar, then cover and cook as instructed above. Enjoy plain or over rice.

Jalapeño Popper Dip

YIELD 10 to 12 portions **I COOK TIME** 1 hour

Ingredients

2 (8-oz.) packages cream
cheese, softened

1 c. mayonnaise

1 (4-oz.) can chopped fire
roasted green chilies, drained

1 (4-oz.) can diced jalapeño
peppers, drained

1 c. grated Parmesan cheese

Directions

1. Combine all ingredients in slow
cooker and stir.

2. Cover and cook on HIGH for
1 hour, or until dip is warmed
through, stirring often to combine.

Tame this spicy
spread with a
few slices of
bacon, cooked,
crumbled and
stirred in.

Enchilada Dip

YIELD 30 portions **I COOK TIME** 8 hours 30 minutes to 10 hours 30 minutes

Ingredients

- 2 lbs. boneless, skinless chicken thighs
- 1 (10-oz.) can enchilada sauce
- 2 (8-oz.) packages cream cheese, softened and cubed
- 4 c. shredded pepper jack cheese

Directions

1. Combine chicken and enchilada sauce in slow cooker.

2. Cover and cook on LOW for 8 to 10 hours, or until chicken is thoroughly cooked.

3. Shred chicken, add cream cheese and pepper jack to slow cooker, then stir.

4. Cover and cook on LOW for 30 minutes, or until mixture is blended and cheese is melted, stirring twice.

Sweet, Hot and Crazy Bites

YIELD 6 to 8 portions |
COOK TIME 3 to 4 hours

Ingredients

- 2 lbs. boneless, skinless chicken breasts, cut into 2-in. pieces
- ½ c. Johnny's Sweet Hot and Crazy Sauce
- ⅓ c. blue cheese, optional

Directions

1. Add chicken and sauce to slow cooker. Stir.

2. Cover and cook on LOW for 3 to 4 hours.

3. If desired, stir in blue cheese, then serve when melted.

Classic
Hot Wings

SERVINGS 4 portions | **COOK TIME** 2 hours to 2 hours 30 minutes on HIGH or 4 to 5 hours on LOW

Ingredients

Salt, to taste

Pepper, to taste

2 lbs. bone-in, skin-on chicken wings

1 (12-oz.) bottle buffalo wing sauce

2 T. unsalted butter, melted

1 (12-oz.) bottle Italian dressing

Celery, to serve

Carrots, to serve

Blue cheese or ranch dressing, to serve

Directions

1. Salt and pepper wings. Broil in the oven for 5 minutes. Transfer wings to slow cooker and top with hot sauce, butter and Italian dressing.

2. Cover and cook on HIGH for 2 hours to 2 hours 30 minutes or on LOW for 4 to 5 hours.

3. Serve immediately with celery, carrots and dressing or keep on WARM for up to 2 hours.

For prettier presentation, spoon sauce from the slow cooker over finished wings and broil again.

Red, White and Blue
Buffalo Chicken Bites

YIELD 4 portions I **COOK TIME** 2 hours

Ingredients

- 2 boneless, skinless chicken breasts, cut into 2-in. pieces
- 2 T. all-purpose flour
- ⅓ c. buffalo sauce
- ⅓ c. Italian salad dressing
- ¼ c. ranch dressing
- Crumbled blue cheese, to garnish

Directions

1. Place chicken in slow cooker. Sprinkle in flour and toss chicken to coat. Mix buffalo sauce with Italian dressing together and pour into slow cooker. Stir until ingredients are well combined.

2. Cover and cook on LOW for 2 hours.

3. Stir in ranch dressing. Serve topped with blue cheese, if desired.

Bacon Wrapped Dogs

YIELD 32 dogs **I COOK TIME** 3 to 4 hours

you can replace little smokies with hot dogs or brats cut into thirds. you'll need about 10.

Ingredients

- 1 (16-oz.) package bacon, slices cut in half
- 1 (16-oz.) package little smokies
- ½ c. packed brown sugar, plus more for a sweeter taste
- 1 t. dried mustard

Directions

1. Wrap bacon around little smokies and secure with toothpicks. Transfer to slow cooker and sprinkle with brown sugar and mustard.

2. Cover and cook on HIGH for 3 to 4 hours, or until bacon is brown.

Easy
Swedish Meatballs

YIELD 6 portions **I** **COOK TIME** 1 hour

Ingredients

3 (16-oz.) bags frozen meatballs, thawed

1 medium red onion, chopped

1 (16-oz.) container sour cream

3 c. brown gravy

1 (4-oz.) package mushrooms, diced

Salt, to taste

Pepper, to taste

⅛ t. garlic powder, optional

Directions

1. Place meatballs and onion in slow cooker. Add sour cream, gravy and mushrooms. Add desired spices and stir.

2. Cover and cook on HIGH for 1 hour, or until meatballs are cooked all the way through.

Make your own meatballs with 3 lbs. ground beef, 3 eggs and 9 T. dry bread crumbs. Bake at 400 degrees F for 15 to 20 minutes.

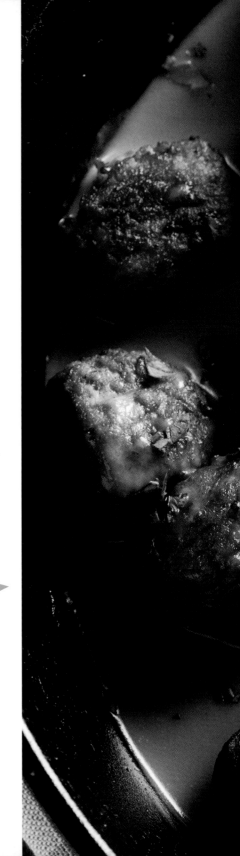

Chili Cheese Dip

YIELD 8 to 10 portions **I COOK TIME** 3 hours

Ingredients

2 c. chili

2 c. shredded cheddar cheese

1 c. milk

3 large green onions, chopped

1 (8-oz.) package cream cheese

Directions

1. Combine all ingredients in slow cooker.

2. Cover and cook on LOW for 3 hours, stirring every 30 minutes.

3. Reduce heat to LOW and serve.

≫ Suggested Servings

Corn chips and chili cheese dip were made for each other. In addition to serving them alongside this irresistible spread, I occasionally crush corn chips and stir them into this recipe before I serve it. The crunch is unbeatable!

Black Bean Dip

YIELD 4 to 6 portions **I COOK TIME** 1 to 2 hours

Who doesn't love pork and beans? Stir in some cooked ham to transform this dip.

Ingredients

3 cloves garlic

1 small yellow onion

1–3 jalapeño peppers

2 (15-oz.) cans black beans

Water, as needed

Ground cumin, to taste

Directions

1. Add garlic, onion, jalapeños and black beans to a food processor. Process until smooth, adding water as needed. Stir in cumin, if desired. Transfer mixture to slow cooker.

2. Cover and cook on LOW for 1 to 2 hours, adding water as needed so the dip keeps its consistency.

Bavarian Meatballs

YIELD 12 portions **I COOK TIME** 3 hours 30 minutes to 4 hours

Ingredients

- 2 dozen frozen Italian-style meatballs, thawed
- 1 small yellow onion, chopped
- ¼ c. packed brown sugar
- 1 (1-oz.) envelope onion soup mix
- 1 (12-oz.) beer

Directions

1. Mix all ingredients in slow cooker.

2. Cover and cook on LOW for 3 hours 30 minutes to 4 hours, or until meatballs are heated through.

Cheeseburger Party Dip

YIELD 7 cups **I COOK TIME** 30 minutes

Ingredients

- 1 lb. ground beef
- 1 (8-oz.) package mushrooms, sliced
- 1 small white onion, diced
- 1 ½ lbs. Velveeta, cubed
- 1 (10-oz.) can diced Rotel

Directions

1. Heat beef, mushrooms and onion in a skillet over medium until beef is browned and vegetables are tender. Drain.

2. Add Velveeta to slow cooker and cook on HIGH until the cheese melts.

3. Add cooked beef, mushrooms, onions and Rotel to slow cooker. Stir until well combined. Cover and cook on HIGH for 30 minutes.

4. Reduce heat to WARM and serve dip from slow cooker, stirring often.

Enjoy this dip with tortilla chips, toasted bread or crackers.

Classic Hummus

YIELD 12 portions **I COOK TIME** 14 to 16 hours

Tastes great with pita bread, pretzels or veggies!

Ingredients

1 (16-oz.) package dried garbanzo beans

4 c. chicken or vegetable broth

1 lemon, juiced

2 cloves garlic, pressed

Paprika, to garnish

Olive oil, to garnish

Directions

1. Rinse garbanzo beans. Combine beans and broth in slow cooker.

2. Cover and cook on WARM for 8 hours

3. Add more warm water to cover beans.

4. Cover and cook on HIGH for 6 to 8 hours. As beans plump and soften, add lemon juice and garlic.

5. Blend mixture in batches, adding water as needed until hummus reaches a desirable consistency.

6. Garnish with paprika and olive oil, then serve.

Cinnamon Apple Martinis

YIELD 8 portions |
COOK TIME 1 to 2 hours

Ingredients

- 3 c. apple juice
- 2 cinnamon sticks
- 1 c. vanilla vodka
   Ground cinnamon, to garnish
   Sugar, to garnish
- 1 apple, sliced, to garnish

Directions

1. Place apple juice and cinnamon sticks in slow cooker.

2. Cover and cook on HIGH for 1 to 2 hours, or until juice is very hot.

3. Add vanilla vodka, stir and reduce heat to WARM.

4. Combine cinnamon and sugar in a shallow bowl. Wet rims of martini glasses and dip into cinnamon-sugar mix. Carefully ladle apple martini mixture into prepared glasses and serve garnished with apple slices, if desired.

Candy Apple Martinis are another favorite. Remove sugar and cinnamon and add sour apple schnapps, instead.

Creamy
Chocolate Fondue

YIELD 8 portions **I COOK TIME** 30 minutes

Ingredients

3　c. semisweet chocolate chips

½　c. white Karo syrup

1　t. pure vanilla extract

2　c. half-and-half

Directions

1. Place chocolate, syrup and vanilla in slow cooker.

2. Cook, uncovered, on HIGH for 30 minutes, stirring frequently.

3. When all the chocolate has melted, add half-and-half a little at a time.

4. Turn slow cooker to LOW and serve.

⟩⟩ Tricks of the Trade

Fondue is simple in theory, but execution is everything. Make sure to brush fresh fruit with lemon juice to prevent it from browning. Additionally, have extra half-and-half on hand and use it to thin out the fondue as it thickens over time.

Beef
Nachos

SERVINGS 12 portions **I** **COOK TIME** 1 hour

Ingredients

1   lb. ground beef

1   small yellow onion, diced, optional

1   (16-oz.) bottle taco sauce

1   (10-oz.) can cream of mushroom soup, optional

1   (16-oz.) can refried beans

2   T. taco seasoning

2   c. shredded Mexican cheese blend

    Tortilla chips, to serve

Directions

1. Brown beef and onion, if using, in a skillet over medium heat. Drain and transfer to slow cooker.

2. Add remaining ingredients to slow cooker.

3. Cover and cook on HIGH for 1 hour, or until mixture is hot and cheese is melted.

4. Spoon mixture over tortilla chips and serve.

Dress these up with black olives, tomatoes, guacamole and anything else you might be craving.

Hot Reuben Spread

YIELD 25 portions **I** **COOK TIME** 2 hours

Serving this dip with rye bread or crackers is a must!

Ingredients

- 2 c. shredded Swiss cheese
- 2 c. sauerkraut, drained
- ⅓ c. Thousand Island dressing
- 1 (8-oz.) package cream cheese, softened
- 2 c. shredded corned beef, cooked

Directions

1. Combine all ingredients in slow cooker.

2. Cover and cook on LOW for 1 hour, or until cheese is melted. Stir until cheese is smooth, cover and cook on LOW for 1 additional hour.

3. Scrape sides of slow cooker with a rubber spatula and stir mixture. Serve directly from slow cooker and remove after 2 hours.

Mexican Corn Dip

YIELD 8 to 10 portions **|**
COOK TIME 1 hour

Ingredients

- 2 (8-oz.) packages cream cheese, softened
- 1 c. butter, softened
- 2 (15 ¼-oz.) cans white corn, drained
- 2 (10-oz.) cans Rotel
- 1 T. chili powder

Directions

1. Combine all ingredients in slow cooker.

2. Cover and cook on LOW for 1 hour, or until all ingredients have melted, stirring often.

Sidekicks

From mashed potatoes to mac and cheese, there's something for everyone in this superb selection of sides.

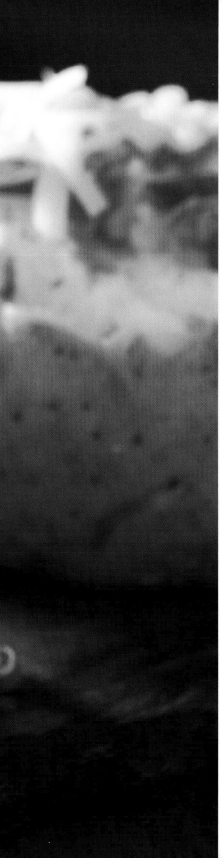

Flawless
Baked Potatoes

YIELD 6 portions **I COOK TIME** 8 hours

Ingredients

6 medium baking potatoes

Olive oil, to coat

Salt, to taste

Pepper, to taste

Butter, to taste

Parmesan cheese, to taste

Directions

1. Wash and pierce potatoes. Coat in olive oil and salt, then wrap in foil and transfer to slow cooker.

2. Cover and cook on LOW for 8 hours.

3. Unwrap potatoes. Slice each lengthwise and top with salt, pepper, butter and cheese, as desired.

Serve potatoes bar-style and allow diners to top them as they please.

Southern
Creamed Corn

YIELD 8 portions **I COOK TIME** 2 to 4 on HIGH or 5 to 6 hours on LOW

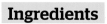

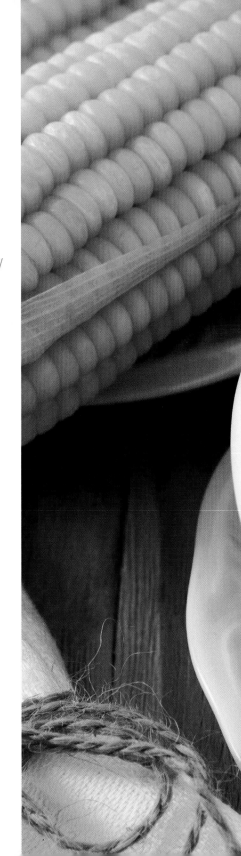

Ingredients

- 1 (20-oz.) bag frozen white corn, thawed
- ½ c. half-and-half
- 1 (8-oz.) package cream cheese, cubed
- ½ c. butter
- 1 T. sugar
- Pepper, to taste

Directions

1. Pour all but 1 c. corn into slow cooker.

2. Pulse 1 c. corn and half-and-half in a blender, then transfer to slow cooker. Combine remaining ingredients. Stir into slow cooker.

3. Cover and cook on HIGH for 2 to 4 hours or on LOW for 5 to 6 hours.

⟫ Au Naturel

Want to sub in fresh corn? Scrape kernels from about 8 large ears with a sharp knife. Slice off the stem to create a flat base. Hold each ear, tip up, then cut downward, removing a few rows at a time. Discard cobs.

Ranch Potatoes

YIELD 6 to 8 portions **I**
COOK TIME 7 hours

Ingredients

2 ½ lbs. small potatoes,
      quartered

1 (1-oz.) envelope buttermilk
    ranch dressing mix

1 (10 ¾-oz.) can cream of
    chicken soup

   Salt, to taste

   Pepper, to taste

1 (8-oz.) package sour cream

Directions

1. Put potatoes in slow cooker.

2. Mix remaining ingredients
(except sour cream) in a bowl,
transfer to slow cooker and stir.

3. Cover and cook on LOW for
6 hours.

4. Stir in sour cream, cover and
cook on LOW for 1 hour.

Red Kidney Beans and Rice

YIELD 4 to 6 portions **I** **COOK TIME** 6 or 8 hours

Chopped jalapeños and celery make great add-ins.

Ingredients

- 1 (16-oz.) bag dry red kidney beans
- 2 c. water
- 4 c. white rice, cooked
- 1 lb. smoked sausage, sliced

  Garlic powder, optional

  Smoked paprika, optional
- 1 large yellow onion, optional

Directions

1. Soak kidney beans for about 8 hours. Rinse and transfer to slow cooker. Add water.

2. Cover and cook on HIGH for 5 hours or on LOW for 7 hours.

3. Add rice and sausage to slow cooker, along with remaining ingredients, if desired.

4. Cover and cook on HIGH for 1 hour.

Cauliflower Garlic Mashed Fauxtatoes

YIELD 6 portions **I COOK TIME** 4 to 6 hours

Ingredients

2 (10-oz.) bags cauliflower florets, washed and drained

3 c. chicken or vegetable broth

4 cloves garlic

1 bay leaf

1 T. unsalted butter

Salt, to taste

Pepper, to taste

Directions

1. Add cauliflower, broth, garlic and bay leaf to slow cooker.

2. Cover and cook on LOW for 4 to 6 hours.

3. Remove bay leaf. Drain broth into a container and set aside.

4. Add butter to cauliflower. Blend cauliflower until smooth. Add reserved broth, 1 T. at a time, until mixture is smooth and creamy.

5. Add salt and pepper, to taste, then serve.

Top these false spuds with fresh herbs for even more flavor.

Dijon Mustard
Brussels Sprouts

YIELD 4 to 6 portions **I COOK TIME** 2 to 3 hours

Ingredients

1   (16-oz.) bag frozen Brussels
    sprouts, thawed

2   T. unsalted butter

2   T. Dijon mustard

1   T. honey or agave nectar

¼   t. salt

¼   t. pepper

¼   c. water

Directions

1. Combine all ingredients in
   slow cooker.

2. Cover and cook on HIGH 2 to
   3 hours.

3. Stir well, then serve.

*In a pinch, you
can sub 3. T honey
mustard for Dijon
and agave.*

Traditional
Macaroni and Cheese

YIELD 6 portions **I COOK TIME** 2 hours 30 minutes

Ingredients

- 2 c. macaroni
- 1 c. shredded cheddar cheese
- ½ c. shredded Swiss cheese
- 4 T. butter
- 1 c. cream or half-and-half

Directions

1. Cook macaroni according to package directions.

2. Add ½ the macaroni to greased slow cooker. Top with ½ the cheddar cheese, ½ the Swiss cheese and 2 t. butter. Repeat layers until ingredients are gone, then add cream or half-and-half.

3. Cover and cook on LOW for 2 hours 30 minutes.

⟫ Secret Ingredient

Add 1 (10 ¾-oz.) can of condensed tomato soup into the slow cooker with the cream or half-and-half to make this recipe even more delicious. The soup makes for a creamier texture and a richer, more unique flavor.

Cheesy
Bacon Potatoes

YIELD 8 to 10 portions | **COOK TIME** 4 to 6 hours

Ingredients

1 medium white onion, thinly sliced

3 green onions, sliced, optional

6 medium potatoes, washed and sliced

1 (16-oz.) package shredded cheddar cheese

½ lb. bacon, cooked and chopped

4 T. butter

Salt, to taste

Pepper, to taste

Directions

1. Add onions, potatoes, cheese and bacon to greased slow cooker in 3 layers. Add butter, salt and pepper.

2. Cover and cook on LOW for 4 to 6 hours.

Stir in 1 can of mushroom soup to make this side more like a casserole.

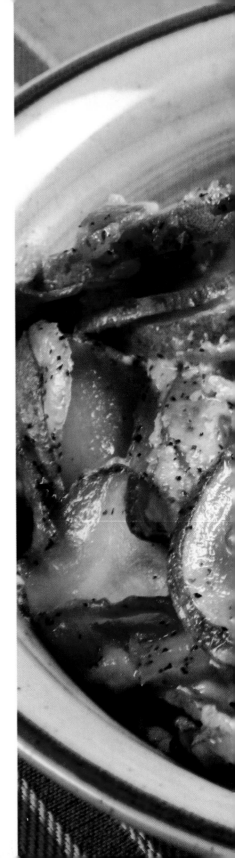

Collard Greens and Ham

YIELD 8 portions I **COOK TIME** 8 hours

Ingredients

4 bunches collard greens or kale, rinsed, trimmed and chopped

1 medium yellow onion, diced

2 c. diced ham steak

2-3 c. chicken broth

1 t. olive oil

Pepper, to taste

Garlic powder, to taste

Directions

1. Fill slow cooker with ½ the collard greens, ½ the onion and ½ the ham. Repeat layers, then fill slow cooker with just enough broth to cover ingredients.

2. Cover and cook on HIGH for 1 hour, or until greens begin to wilt.

3. Stir in olive oil, pepper and garlic powder.

4. Cover and bring to a boil on HIGH. Then reduce heat to LOW for 7 hours.

Collards go great with pulled pork. Try the recipe on page 204!

Green Bean Casserole

YIELD 6 to 8 portions **| COOK TIME** 5 to 6 hours

Ingredients

- 2 (10-oz.) bags frozen green beans
- 1 (14 ¾-oz.) can cream of mushroom soup
- ⅓ c. milk
- ¼ t. salt
- ¼ t. pepper
- 1 (2.8-oz.) can French-fried onions

Directions

1. Combine all ingredients (except a handful of French-fried onions) to slow cooker.

2. Cover and cook on LOW for 5 to 6 hours.

3. Top with remaining onions and serve.

For a healthier take, you can replace fried onions with the fresh sautéed variety.

Sweet
Brown Sugar Potatoes

you'll never regret that extra pat of butter on top!

YIELD 6 portions **I** **COOK TIME** 7 hours

Ingredients

4–6 medium sweet potatoes, peeled and sliced

Salt, to taste

1 c. packed brown sugar

3 T. cornstarch

1 t. ground cinnamon

2 T. butter

Pecans or walnuts, to garnish

Directions

1. Add sliced sweet potatoes to greased slow cooker. Sprinkle with salt, brown sugar, cornstarch and cinnamon. Dot with butter.

2. Cover and cook on LOW for 7 hours.

3. Garnish with nuts, if desired, and serve.

German
Potato Salad

YIELD 4 to 5 portions **I COOK TIME** 5 to 6 hours

Ingredients

4   medium potatoes, peeled and sliced

1   medium red onion, diced

¼   c. apple cider vinegar

3   T. olive oil

2   t. Dijon mustard

1   T. sugar, optional

Salt, to taste

Pepper, to taste

Chopped parsley, to garnish

5   slices bacon, cooked and crumbled, to garnish

Directions

1. Combine all ingredients (except garnishes) in slow cooker and stir.

2. Cover and cook on LOW for 5 to 6 hours.

3. Garnish with parsley and bacon, then serve.

This side tastes great hot, cold or at room temperature.

Easiest
Lemon Broccoli

YIELD 6 to 8 portions | **COOK TIME** 1 hour

Ingredients

- 1 (16-oz.) bag broccoli florets, cut into bite-sized pieces
- ½ c. water
- ¼ c. white wine, any variety
- Salt, to taste
- 1 lemon, zested and juiced
- Pepper, to taste

Directions

1. Add broccoli, water, wine and salt to slow cooker and stir.

2. Cover and cook on HIGH for 1 hour, or until broccoli is tender.

3. Stir in lemon zest and juice, more salt and pepper, to taste, then serve.

Breakfast All Week

Make use of leftovers by transferring them to muffin tins, topping with whisked eggs and baking at 350 degrees F for 20 minutes. Refrigerate in a zip-top bag for up to 1 week. Two c. broccoli and 10 eggs will yield 12 muffins.

Cheesy Cauliflower and Broccoli

YIELD 6 to 8 portions **I COOK TIME** 5 hours

Ingredients

- 4 slices bacon, cooked and crumbled
- 2 c. cauliflower florets
- 2 c. broccoli florets
- 1 (10-¾-oz.) can cheddar cheese soup
- Salt, to taste
- Pepper, to taste
- ½ c. grated Parmesan cheese

Directions

1. Add broccoli and cauliflower to slow cooker. Top with soup, bacon, salt and pepper.

2. Cover and cook on LOW for 5 hours.

3. Top with cheddar cheese and serve when melted.

Pack a little more protein—and flavor—into this dish by stirring in 1 c. cooked ham or bacon.

Simple
Spaghetti Squash

YIELD 4 to 5 portions **I** **COOK TIME** 2 hours 30 minutes

Ingredients

1   medium spaghetti squash

½ c. water

2-4 T. butter or margarine, optional

    Salt, to taste

    Pepper, to taste

Directions

1. Place a whole spaghetti squash in slow cooker with water.

2. Cover and cook on HIGH for 2 hours 30 minutes.

3. Carefully remove squash from slow cooker and slice in half, lengthwise. Allow squash to cool slightly before removing seeds. Starting from the outside, scrape squash with a fork.

4. Add spaghetti squash, butter, salt and pepper to small bowl. Stir and serve.

Serve with meatballs to make this side a main course!

Zesty Italian
Red Potatoes

YIELD 8 portions **I** **COOK TIME** 4 hours on HIGH or 8 hours on LOW

Ingredients

24 small, red potatoes, cubed

2 T. olive oil

1 (1-oz.) envelope zesty Italian dressing mix

Sliced green peppers, to garnish, optional

Directions

1. Combine potatoes, olive oil and dressing mix in a plastic zip-top bag. Shake to coat, then transfer potatoes to slow cooker.

2. Cover and cook on HIGH for 4 hours or on LOW for 8 hours. Garnish with peppers and serve.

⫸ Make It A Salad

Turning this recipe into good old-fashioned potato salad is simple: Just add 6 chopped hard boiled eggs, 3. c mayonnaise, 1 diced stalk of celery and 1 diced yellow onion to room temperature potatoes, stir and serve!

Deep South
Green Beans

YIELD 4 to 6 portions **I** **COOK TIME** 4 hours 30 minutes

Ingredients

½ lb. ham, cooked and cut into chunks

4 medium yellow onions, sliced

1 (32-oz.) bag frozen green beans

2 (14 ½-oz.) cans stewed Italian recipe tomatoes, drained

½ t. salt

¼ t. pepper

Directions

1. Combine all ingredients in slow cooker and stir.

2. Cover and cook on LOW for 4 hours 30 minutes.

Subbing bacon in this recipe is just as delicious.

Mashed Potatoes

YIELD 8 portions **I COOK TIME** 2 hours

For smoother potatoes, use a hand mixer instead of a potato masher.

Ingredients

- 4 lbs. red potatoes, cut into chunks
- 2 cloves garlic, minced, optional
- 1 (32-oz.) container chicken broth
- 1 (8-oz.) container sour cream
- 1 (8-oz.) package herbed cream cheese, softened
- ½ c. butter
- Salt, to taste
- Pepper, to taste

Directions

1. Cook potatoes, garlic, if using, and broth in a pot of lightly salted boiling water until potatoes are tender but firm, about 15 minutes. Drain, reserving liquid.

2. In a bowl, mash potatoes with sour cream and cream cheese, adding reserved liquid as needed to attain desired consistency.

3. Transfer mixture to slow cooker.

4. Cover and cook on LOW for 2 hours, stirring once halfway through cooking.

5. Stir in butter, salt and pepper, then serve.

Thai Curry Spaghetti Squash

YIELD 4 portions **|**
COOK TIME 5 to 6 hours

Ingredients

1   medium spaghetti squash

1   (13 ½-oz.) can full-fat coconut milk, at room temperature

1–2 T. red curry paste

¼ cup water

4–6 cloves garlic, optional

Directions

1. Cut spaghetti squash in half, lengthwise. Remove seeds and poke holes in tops of both halves. Set aside.

2. Pour coconut milk, curry paste, water and garlic, if desired, into slow cooker. Add squash halves, cut-side down.

3. Cover and cook on LOW for 4 to 5 hours, or until squash is softened to your liking.

4. Remove and allow squash to cool slightly. Starting from the outside, scrape squash with a fork.

5. Pour desired amount of coconut curry sauce from slow cooker over squash spaghetti and serve.

Leftover noodles can be frozen in zip-top bags.

Sidekicks

Kale and Beans

YIELD 6 portions **I** **COOK TIME** 3 hours on HIGH or 4 hours on LOW

Ingredients

1   (10-oz.) container chopped baby kale

2   c. green beans

1   (5 ½-oz.) can coconut milk

1   (14-oz.) can chicken broth

1   t. yellow curry powder

Directions

1. Combine all ingredients in slow cooker and stir.

2. Cover and cook on HIGH for 3 hours or on LOW for 4.

Add more kale, mushrooms and Parmesan cheese to make this side more like a salad.

Au Gratin Potatoes

YIELD 8 to 10 portions **I COOK TIME** 5 hours

Ingredients

6   large russet potatoes, peeled and thinly sliced

8   slices bacon, cooked and crumbled, optional

    Salt, to taste

    Pepper, to taste

3   c. half-and-half

4   T. all-purpose flour

½   c. freshly grated white cheddar cheese

Directions

1. Layer potatoes and bacon, if using, in slow cooker, adding salt and pepper between layers.

2. Add half-and-half to a small saucepan and heat on medium. Once warm, whisk in flour until there are no lumps. Add cheese and whisk for 1 to 2 minutes, or until cheese is melted. Pour mixture into slow cooker.

3. Cover and cook on LOW for 5 hours.

Finish slow-cooked potatoes in the broiler for a crispy charred top.

Creamy
Asparagus Casserole

YIELD 8 to 10 portions **I COOK TIME** 4 to 5 hours

Ingredients

- 2 (10-oz.) cans sliced asparagus, drained
- 1 (10-oz.) can cream of celery soup
- 2 hard boiled eggs, thinly sliced, optional
- 15 saltine crackers, crushed
- 1 t. butter
- 1 c. shredded cheddar cheese

Directions

1. Add asparagus to lightly greased slow cooker.

2. In a bowl, combine soup and eggs, if using. Top with crackers and butter. Pour into slow cooker.

3. Cover and cook on LOW for 4 to 5 hours.

4. Add cheese, cover and cook on LOW just until melted.

⫸ Crunchy Casserole

If you prefer a crispier casserole, combine 1 c. cracker crumbs with 4 T. softened butter. Sprinkle mixture over asparagus when adding cheese in the final step and cook until topping is golden brown.

Superior Soups

Whether you're hoping to lighten up lunchtime or round out your dinner menu, these bowls are just the ticket.

Broccoli Cheddar Soup

YIELD 8 portions | **COOK TIME** 6 hours

Ingredients

- 2 T. olive oil
- ¼ c. whole wheat flour
- 4 c. chicken or vegetable broth
- 1 (10-oz.) bag frozen broccoli, thawed
  Salt, to taste
  Pepper, to taste
- 1 clove garlic, minced, optional
- 3 c. shredded cheddar cheese, divided

Directions

1. Place olive oil in a skillet and whisk in flour. Add broth and whisk until there are no lumps.

2. Pour mixture into slow cooker. Add broccoli, salt, pepper and garlic, if using.

3. Cover and cook on LOW for 6 hours.

4. In small batches, blend soup until it reaches a desirable texture and thickness.

5. Add 2 ½ c. cheddar cheese. Stir cheese until melted and well mixed. Garnish with remaining cheese, if desired, and serve.

Serve with crusty bread or savory scones.

Superior Soups

Busy Working Mom's
BBQ Chili

YIELD 8 portions **I** **COOK TIME** 8 to 10 hours

Ingredients

½ T. olive oil

1 Vidalia onion, chopped

1½-2 lbs. ground beef

1 (22-oz.) can BBQ baked beans

1 (1-oz.) envelope chili seasoning

Directions

1. Add olive oil and onion to a large skillet and cook for 1 to 2 minutes. Add beef and cook until brown. Drain excess grease.

2. Transfer mixture to a slow cooker. Add remaining ingredients and stir.

3. Cover and cook on LOW for 8 to 10 hours.

⫸ BBQ Or Bust

To amp up flavor, add 1 c. BBQ sauce. You can also use pulled pork in place of ground beef to give this chili a more authentic feel. Big thanks to loyal reader Beth Krajewski Devans for sending this recipe in!

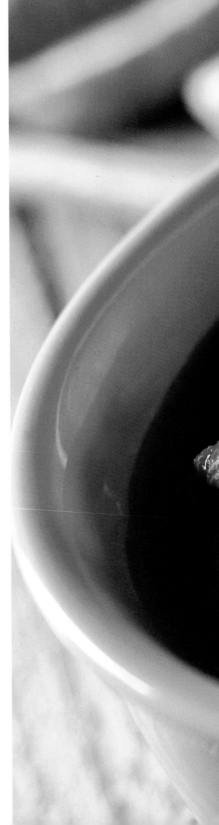

Squash and Apple Bisque

YIELD 8 portions **I** **COOK TIME** 3 hours 15 minutes to 5 hours 15 minutes on HIGH or 8 hours 15 minutes to 10 hours 15 minutes on LOW

Ingredients

- 2 lbs. butternut squash, peeled and cubed
- 1 (14 ½-oz.) can chicken broth
- 3 medium apples, peeled and sliced
- 1 t. ground ginger
- ¼ t. salt
- 1 small yellow onion, chopped, optional
- ½ c. sour cream, at room temperature

Directions

1. Mix all ingredients (except sour cream) in slow cooker.

2. Cover and cook on HIGH for 3 to 5 hours, on LOW for 8 to 10 hours or until squash is tender.

3. Transfer mixture to a blender in small batches and blend until smooth. Return soup to slow cooker and stir in sour cream.

4. Cover and cook on LOW for 15 minutes, or until soup is hot, and serve.

Garnish with more sour cream, if desired.

15-Bean Corned Beef Stew

YIELD 12 portions **I** **COOK TIME** 14 hours

Ingredients

- 1 (20-oz.) package Hurst's HamBeens® 15 Bean Soup®
- 3 lbs. corned beef
- 1 medium yellow onion, chopped
- 3 cloves garlic
- Salt, to taste
- Pepper, to taste
- 1 (12-oz.) bottle Guinness

Directions

1. Rinse and sort beans, then transfer to slow cooker. Cover with 3 c. water.

2. Cover and cook on LOW for 7 hours.

3. Place corned beef in separate slow cooker. Top with chopped onion, garlic, salt, pepper and beer.

4. Cover and cook on LOW for 6 hours.

5. Remove beef from slow cooker and shred, reserving liquid accumulated at the bottom of slow cooker. Add shredded corned beef to the bean-filled slow cooker and stir. Add reserved liquid and stir.

6. Cover and cook on LOW for 1 hour.

Oyster Soup

YIELD 8 to 10 portions **I** **COOK TIME** 4 to 5 hours

Sub cream in place of milk for a richer taste.

Ingredients

- 6 c. milk
- 2 T. all-purpose flour
- 2 T. water, optional
- ¼ c. butter
- 1 t. Worcestershire sauce
- Salt, to taste
- Pepper, to taste
- 1 t. cayenne pepper, optional
- 2 (8-oz.) cans oysters with liquid

Directions

1. Add all ingredients (except oysters) to slow cooker. Stir.

2. Cover and cook on HIGH for 2 hours.

3. Stir, then add oysters.

4. Cover and cook on LOW for 2 to 3 hours.

Superior Soups

Chicken and Corn Chili

YIELD 6 portions |
COOK TIME 4 hours 30 minutes to 5 hours 30 minutes

Ingredients

1 ½   lbs. boneless, skinless chicken breast

1   (16-oz.) jar salsa

1   (15-oz.) can black beans, drained and rinsed

1   t. garlic salt, optional

1   t. ground cumin, optional

1   t. chili powder, optional

¼   t. pepper, optional

1   (15 ¼-oz.) can Del Monte fiesta corn

Directions

1. Add chicken to slow cooker.

2. In a medium bowl, combine the remaining ingredients (except the corn) and transfer the mixture to slow cooker.

3. Cover and cook on LOW for 4 to 5 hours.

4. Remove chicken and shred. Return the chicken to slow cooker and stir.

5. Stir in corn, cover and cook on LOW for 30 minutes.

This corn-filled dish pairs particularly well with cornbread.

Easy
Cream of Broccoli Soup

YIELD 6 portions **I COOK TIME** 5 hours 15 minutes

Ingredients

1 large potato, peeled and cubed

1 large yellow onion, cut into large cubes

7 c. chicken stock

Salt, to taste

Pepper, to taste

5 c. broccoli, chopped

¾ c. half-and-half

Ground nutmeg, to taste, optional

Directions

1. Place the potatoes, onions, chicken stock, salt and pepper in slow cooker.

2. Cover and cook on HIGH for 4 hours.

3. Stir in broccoli, cover and cook on HIGH for 1 hour.

4. Stir in half-and-half, cover and cook on HIGH for 15 minutes.

5. Ladle ½ the soup into a blender and pulse until smooth. Return to slow cooker and stir. Taste, season with salt, pepper and nutmeg, if desired, then serve.

For a chunkier soup, forget the blender.

Loaded
Baked Potato Soup

YIELD 8 portions **I** **COOK TIME** 6 to 8 hours

Ingredients

1 (32-oz.) bag frozen shredded hash browns

3 (14-oz.) cans chicken broth

1 (10 ¾-oz.) can cream of chicken soup

1 small yellow onion, chopped

Pepper, to taste

1 (8-oz.) package cream cheese

Directions

1. Combine everything (except the cream cheese) in slow cooker.

2. Cover and cook on LOW for 6 to 8 hours.

3. About 1 hour before soup is finished cooking, add cream cheese, stirring occasionally.

≫ Make It Your Own

The great thing about the recipes in this book is that they are adaptable to match your tastes and work as a starting point for more complex dishes. Add bacon, cheese, scallions, sour cream or other ingredients to this recipe as you see fit.

The Main Event

You'll never lose sleep—or time—with these recipes.
Five ingredients, one pot and dinner is done.

Garlic Shrimp Scampi

YIELD 4 to 6 portions **I COOK TIME** 1 hour 20 minutes

Ingredients

½ (16-oz.) package angel hair pasta

1 ½ c. white wine

2 large shallots, finely chopped, optional

1 c. chicken stock

6 T. Johnny's Garlic Spread

1 T. lemon juice, optional

2 lbs. raw shrimp, peeled and deveined

Directions

1. Add all ingredients (except the shrimp) to slow cooker.

2. Cover and cook on HIGH for 1 hour.

3. Stir in shrimp.

4. Cover and cook for 20 minutes, or until shrimp are cooked.

>> Wine Substitute

If you prefer to cook without alcohol, you can use white wine vinegar, lemon juice, white grape juice or vegetable stock, instead. I prefer the vinegar best because it packs all the flavor of white wine without the alcohol.

BBQ Peach Chicken

YIELD 4 portions **I COOK TIME** 3 to 4 on HIGH or 6 to 8 hours on LOW

Ingredients

2–3 lbs. skinless chicken drumsticks

1 c. BBQ sauce

⅓ c. peach jam

2 t. Dijon mustard

Directions

1. Combine all ingredients in slow cooker until chicken is coated in sauce.

2. Cover and cook on HIGH for 3 to 4 hours or on LOW for 6 to 8 hours.

3. Transfer chicken to a serving platter and cover. Transfer liquid from slow cooker to a saucepan and bring to a slight boil over medium heat. Reduce heat to low and simmer for about 10 minutes, or until the sauce reaches a desirable consistency.

4. Pour the sauce over the chicken and serve.

Homestyle
Chicken and Noodles

YIELD 8 portions I **COOK TIME** 8 hours

Make this dish thicker by stirring in flour.

Ingredients

4 lbs. boneless, skinless chicken breasts, chunked

Salt, to taste

Pepper, to taste

Garlic powder, to taste

3 (10 ¾-oz.) cans cream of chicken soup

2 (32-oz.) containers chicken broth

2 (12-oz.) packages frozen egg noodles

Directions

1. Coat chicken breast with salt, pepper and garlic powder, then transfer to slow cooker.

2. In a separate bowl, combine soup and chicken broth, then pour mixture over chicken.

3. Cover and cook on LOW for 8 hours.

4. Add noodles 2 hours before serving. Turn slow cooker to HIGH and stir occasionally, every 20 to 30 minutes.

The Main Event

Asian Chicken

YIELD 6 portions **I COOK TIME** 5 to 6 hours

Serve chicken with reduced liquid from the slow cooker.

Ingredients

- 6 chicken leg quarters
- ½ c. soy sauce
- ¼ c. packed light brown sugar
- ½ t. garlic powder
- 1 (8-oz.) can tomato sauce

Directions

1. Place chicken pieces in slow cooker. Combine remaining ingredients in a bowl and pour over chicken.

2. Cover and cook on LOW for 5 to 6 hours, or until chicken is tender and juices run clear.

Pizza Pork Chops

YIELD 6 portions **I COOK TIME** 4 to 6 hours

Ingredients

2 ¼ lbs. (1 in.-thick) pork loin chops

½ t. salt

¼ t. pepper

1 T. vegetable oil

2 c. marinara sauce

1 medium yellow onion, chopped, optional

1 clove garlic, minced, optional

4 c. orzo, cooked

1 c. shredded mozzarella cheese

Directions

1. Season pork chops with salt and pepper and cook in a large skillet with oil over medium heat for about 4 minutes.

2. Transfer pork to slow cooker. Add marinara, followed by onion and garlic, if desired.

3. Cover and cook on LOW for 4 to 6 hours.

4. Serve pork over cooked orzo. Top with sauce from slow cooker and mozzarella cheese.

Add pepperoni for a delicious and pizza-themed garnish.

Bacon-Wrapped Apple Chicken

YIELD 6 portions **I COOK TIME** 8 hours

Ingredients

- 2 lbs. boneless, skinless chicken breasts
- 16 bacon slices
- 2 c. BBQ sauce
- 2 Granny Smith apples, peeled and diced
- 1 lemon, juiced

Directions

1. Wrap 2 to 3 slices of bacon around each chicken breast, then transfer to slow cooker.

2. Top with BBQ sauce, apples and lemon juice.

3. Cover and cook on LOW for 8 hours.

Coffee-Cooked
Venison Roast

YIELD 6 to 8 portions **I** **COOK TIME** 7 to 8 hours

Ingredients

2–3 lbs. venison roast

1 ⅓ c. brewed coffee

1 (10 ½-oz.) can cream of mushroom soup

1 ½ (2-oz.) envelopes onion soup mix

1 t. steak seasoning

Directions

1. Place roast in slow cooker. Gradually mix hot coffee with cream of mushroom soup until smooth. Pour over venison. Sprinkle in onion soup mix and steak seasoning.

2. Cover and cook on HIGH for 7 to 8 hours.

Cooked correctly, venison roast should be pinkish and juicy.

Pork Carnitas Tacos

YIELD 12 portions I **COOK TIME** 8 to 10 hours

Ingredients

1   T. chipotle chili powder
2   t. ground cumin
2   t. garlic powder
1 ½   t. salt
1   t. onion powder
3   lbs. boneless pork loin roast
    Taco shells, to serve

Directions

1. Combine all dry ingredients in a small bowl to make a rub. Coat pork with rub and transfer to slow cooker.

2. Cover and cook on LOW for 8 to 10 hours.

3. Shred pork and serve in shells with desired toppings.

>> Taco Night Tip

Making hard-shell tacos is much tastier than buying them. Put flour tortillas in a damp paper towel and microwave for 30 seconds. Coat with oil, drape over the bars of a clean oven rack and cook at 375 degrees F until crisp.

Bloody Mary Chicken

YIELD 10 to 12 portions **I**
COOK TIME 8 hours

Ingredients

4 lbs. boneless, skinless chicken breasts

4 c. bloody mary mix

Directions

1. Combine both ingredients in slow cooker.

2. Cover and cook on LOW for 8 hours.

Cook with 1 c. chopped celery, 1 c. chopped onion and 1 c. chopped carrot to taste.

Classic Lasagna

YIELD 8 portions **I** **COOK TIME** 4 to 6 hours

For lasagna with a kick, use hot or spicy Italian sausage instead of ground beef.

Ingredients

- 1 lb. ground beef
- Salt, to taste
- Pepper, to taste
- 1 (32-oz.) jar marinara sauce
- 1 (24-oz.) container ricotta cheese
- ¼ c. water, optional
- 1 t. garlic powder, optional
- 2 T. Italian seasoning, optional
- 1 (12-oz.) package lasagna noodles, uncooked
- 2 c. shredded mozzarella cheese

Directions

1. Season beef with salt and pepper, then transfer to a skillet over medium-high heat. Cook until brown, then drain. Return beef to skillet and add marinara sauce.

2. In a separate bowl, mix ricotta, water, ¼ t. pepper, ½ t. salt, garlic powder and Italian seasoning.

3. In slow cooker, layer ½ c. sauce, ⅓ of the noodles (broken to fit), ⅓ of the ricotta mixture and ¼ c. mozzarella cheese. Layer two more times with ⅓ of the noodles, ⅓ of ricotta mixture and ¼ c. mozzarella cheese. Add remaining sauce to slow cooker and reserve remaining mozzarella cheese in the refrigerator.

4. Cover and cook on LOW for 4 to 6 hours.

5. Sprinkle remaining mozzarella cheese on top of lasagna and serve when melted.

The Main Event

Butter Beef

YIELD 8 portions **I** **COOK TIME** 8 hours

Serve over noodles to make this a meal.

Ingredients

- 3 lbs. beef chuck
- ½ c. butter
- 1 (2-oz.) envelope onion soup mix
- 1 medium yellow onion, sliced

Directions

1. Put beef in slow cooker and top with remaining ingredients.
2. Cover and cook on LOW for 8 hours. Stir occasionally.

BBQ Turkey

YIELD 6 portions **I**
COOK TIME 3 to 4 hours

Ingredients

2–3 lbs. chopped or shredded turkey

⅛ t. salt

⅛ t. pepper

2 c. BBQ sauce

⅛ t. celery salt

2 green bell peppers, cut into strips, optional

1 small yellow onion, chopped

Directions

1. Place turkey in the bottom of slow cooker and season with salt and pepper.

2. Combine BBQ sauce and celery salt, green peppers and onions. Pour over turkey.

3. Cover and cook on HIGH for 3 to 4 hours.

The Main Event

Coconut-Braised Pork

YIELD 8 to 10 portions **I COOK TIME** 8 hours

Ingredients

- 2 T. olive oil
- 3 lbs. boneless pork shoulder, cut into 2-in. chunks
- ¼ c. fish sauce
- 1-2 c. coconut water
- ½ c. fresh cilantro, coarsely chopped, to garnish
- 2-3 scallions, coarsely chopped, to garnish

Directions

1. Heat oil in a large skillet over medium-high. Sear meat until both sides are brown, about 15 minutes total.

2. Transfer the pork to slow cooker. Add fish sauce and just enough coconut water to nearly cover the meat.

3. Cover and cook on LOW for 8 hours.

4. Serve warm, seasoned with liquid in slow cooker and garnished with cilantro and scallion, if desired.

Further shred pork with forks before serving.

Apple-Butter Ribs

YIELD 4 portions **I COOK TIME** 9 hours

Ingredients

3 lbs. country-style boneless
   pork ribs

¾ t. salt

¼ t. pepper

¾ c. apple butter

3 T. packed brown sugar

2 cloves garlic, finely chopped

1 t. liquid smoke

Directions

1. Rub ribs with salt and pepper, then transfer them to slow cooker.

2. Combine remaining ingredients and pour mixture into slow cooker.

3. Cover and cook on LOW for 9 hours.

Infuse even more apple into
this dish by tossing a few
slices into the slow cooker.

Creamy
Italian Chicken and Rice

YIELD 6 to 8 portions **I COOK TIME** 4 to 6 hours

Ingredients

1 ½   boneless, skinless chicken breasts

1   (8-oz.) package cream cheese, softened

1   (10 ¾-oz.) can cream of chicken soup

1   (1-oz.) envelope Italian dressing seasoning mix

4   c. rice, cooked

Directions

1. Place chicken in bottom of slow cooker. Combine cream cheese, cream of chicken soup and Italian seasoning and pour over the chicken.

2. Cover and cook on HIGH for 4 to 6 hours, or until chicken is tender.

3. Shred chicken and return to slow cooker. Stir and serve over rice.

Beer-Marinated Chicken

YIELD 8 portions **I COOK TIME** 4 to 5 hours

Ingredients

2   lbs. boneless, skinless chicken breasts

1   (12-oz.) bottle light beer

1   t. garlic powder

1   T. dried oregano

½   t. pepper

1   t. salt

Directions

1. Place all ingredients in slow cooker.

2. Cover and cook on HIGH for 4 to 5 hours.

A lighter main means heartier sides. Serve with potatoes, green beans and corn bread.

Maple Brown Sugar Ham

YIELD 12 portions **I COOK TIME** 5 hours

Ingredients

- 1 (8-lb.) spiral-cut ham
- 1 c. packed brown sugar
- ½ c. pure maple syrup
- 2 c. pineapple juice
- 1 t. ground cloves

Directions

1. Place ham in slow cooker.

2. Rub brown sugar over ham. Whisk pineapple juice, maple syrup and cloves in medium bowl, then pour the mixture over the entire ham.

3. Cover and cook on LOW for 4 hours. Flip the ham, cover and cook on LOW for 1 hour.

4. Carefully remove ham from slow cooker. Wait 15 minutes, then carve.

Lemon-Pepper Chicken

YIELD 4 portions I **COOK TIME** 5 to 6 hours

Ingredients

- 2   t. lemon-pepper seasoning
- ½   t. salt
- ¼   t. pepper
- 2   lbs. boneless, skinless chicken breasts or thighs
- ¼   c. water
- 3   T. lemon juice
- 3   cloves garlic, minced
- 1   T. chopped fresh parsley, optional

Directions

1. Mix lemon pepper, salt and pepper in a bowl and rub the mixture onto the chicken. Place chicken in slow cooker.

2. In a small bowl, combine water, lemon juice and garlic. Pour the mixture into slow cooker.

3. Cover and cook on LOW for 5 to 6 hours.

4. Garnish with fresh parsley, if desired, and serve.

⟫ Rule of Chicken

You should only add chicken to the slow cooker after it has been thawed, never while the meat is still frozen. If the poultry is added while frozen, it may cook unevenly and develop harmful bacteria in the process.

The Main Event

Catalina Chicken

YIELD 4 to 5 portions **I COOK TIME** 6 to 8 hours

Tastes great over rice with a mixed green salad on the side.

Ingredients

- 2 lbs. boneless, skinless chicken breasts
- 1 c. apricot jam
- 1 c. Catalina or French dressing
- 1½ (2-oz.) envelopes onion soup mix

Directions

1. Combine all ingredients in slow cooker, making sure chicken is well coated.

2. Cook on LOW for 6 to 8 hours.

Easy
Chicken and Dumplings

YIELD 6 portions **I** **COOK TIME** 4 to 6 hours

Ingredients

- 2 (12 ½-oz.) cans cooked chicken
- 4 (14-oz.) cans chicken broth
- 1 (10 ¾-oz.) can cream of chicken soup
- 3 (12-oz.) cylinders buttermilk biscuits, cut into fourths
- 1 (12-oz.) bag frozen mixed vegetables

Directions

1. Combine canned chicken, chicken broth and cream of chicken soup in slow cooker and stir well. Place biscuits on top and stir slightly until pieces are covered in the mixture.

2. Cover and cook on HIGH for 4 to 6 hours, stirring often so that the biscuits do not stick to the sides of slow cooker. Add mixed vegetables 1 hour before cook time ends and stir.

Chicago-Style
Italian Beef

YIELD 6 to 8 portions **I COOK TIME** 4 to 6 hours on HIGH or 10 to 12 hours on LOW

Ingredients

3–4 lbs. lean rump roast

  2 t. salt

  4 cloves garlic

  2 t. Parmesan cheese

  1 (12-oz.) can beef broth

  1 t. dried oregano, optional

Directions

1. Place roast in slow cooker and cut 4 slits in the top. Fill each slit with ½ t. salt, 1 garlic clove and ½ t. cheese. Pour broth over meat. Sprinkle with oregano, if desired.

2. Cover and cook on HIGH for 4 to 6 hours or on LOW for 10 to 12 hours.

3. Serve with rice and veggies or on a hoagie with your preferred fixings.

Bacon-Wrapped Pork Tenderloin

YIELD 6 to 8 portions **I COOK TIME** 4 hours

Other dark sodas, such as root beer, will work in place of cola.

Ingredients

- 1 medium yellow onion, sliced
- 2–3 lbs. pork tenderloin
- 12 slices bacon, cooked to medium-rare
- 1 (12-oz.) can cola
- 1 (8-oz.) bottle Johnny's French Dip Sauce

Directions

1. Wrap slices of cooked bacon around pork. Place onions and pork in slow cooker. Pour in cola and sauce.

2. Cover and cook on LOW for 4 hours, or until pork reaches an internal temperature of 145 degrees F.

3. Remove pork from slow cooker. Wait 3 minutes, slice and serve with juice from slow cooker.

Pineapple Teriyaki Chicken

YIELD 4 to 6 portions **I COOK TIME** 7 to 9 hours

Serve over rice, dressed up with additional veggies.

Ingredients

1–1 ½ lbs. chicken breast

    Salt, to taste

    Pepper, to taste

1   (8-oz.) can pineapple chunks

2   T. Dijon mustard

2   T. soy sauce

1–2 cloves garlic, minced

Directions

1. Season chicken with salt and pepper, then transfer to slow cooker.

2. Combine remaining ingredients and pour the mixture over chicken.

3. Cover and cook on LOW for 7 to 9 hours.

World's Best BBQ Short Ribs

YIELD 4 to 5 portions **|**
COOK TIME 8 hours

Ingredients

- 1   large yellow onion, sliced
- 1   (12-oz.) bottle BBQ sauce
- 1   (12-oz.) bottle honey Dijon mustard
- 3–4 lbs. pork short ribs, fat and bones removed

Directions

1. Add sliced onions to medium slow cooker. Combine BBQ sauce, mustard and ribs until meat is well coated. Transfer ribs and sauce mixture to slow cooker.

2. Cover and cook on LOW for 8 hours.

Tastes great with baked beans!

The Main Event

Redcurrant Pomegranate Glazed Ham

YIELD 12 portions **I COOK TIME** 4 hours 30 minutes to 6 hours 30 minutes

Buy a spiral-cut ham and save yourself the trouble of carving!

Ingredients

- 1 (6-lb.) bone-in half ham
- 1 c. pomegranate juice
- ½ c. redcurrant or grape jelly
- 2 T. Dijon mustard
- ¼ c. packed dark brown sugar

Directions

1. Place ham in slow cooker and pour pomegranate juice over top.

2. Cover and cook on LOW for 5 hours.

3. Combine 3 T. cooking liquid from slow cooker with jelly, mustard and brown sugar in a small saucepan. Bring to a boil over high heat, stirring until sugar has dissolved.

4. Baste ham with jelly mixture.

5. Cover and cook on HIGH for 30 minutes, basting 2 to 3 times.

Mississippi Roast

YIELD 10 to 12 portions **I COOK TIME** 8 hours

Ingredients

4 lbs. chuck roast

   Pepper, to taste

1 (1-oz.) envelope ranch dressing mix

1 (1 ¼-oz.) envelope au jus gravy mix

½ c. butter

4–5 pepperoncini peppers

Directions

1. Place roast in greased slow cooker and season with pepper. Add ranch dressing and au jus mix. Top with butter and peppers.

2. Cover and cook on LOW for 8 hours.

Serve roast topped with liquid from the slow cooker for a savory, succulent finish.

Cranberry Chicken

YIELD 4 portions **I** **COOK TIME** 8 hours

Ingredients

2   lbs. boneless, skinless chicken breasts

1   (16-oz.) bottle Catalina dressing

1   (2-oz.) envelope onion soup mix

1   (14-oz.) can cranberry sauce

Directions

1. Place chicken breasts in slow cooker and top with dressing, soup mix and cranberry sauce.

2. Cover and cook on LOW for 8 hours.

⟫ Homemade Sauce

Making cranberry sauce in the slow cooker is easy. All you need is 1 ½ c. cranberries, ½ c. orange juice, ½ c. water and ¼ c. sugar (or more for your taste). Add ingredients to slow cooker, cover and cook on HIGH for 3 to 4 hours.

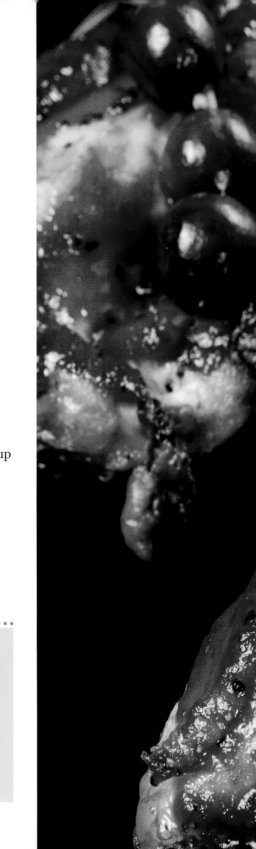

Teriyaki Ginger Pork Chops

YIELD 4 portions **I**
COOK TIME 6 to 7 hours

Ingredients

- ⅔ cup teriyaki sauce
- 1 T. packed brown sugar
- 1 t. fresh minced ginger
- 4 pork loin chops
- 3 T. chopped scallions

Directions

1. Combine teriyaki, brown sugar and ginger in a gallon-sized plastic bag with the chops. Seal and refrigerate overnight, or for about 8 hours.

2. Place pork chops and sauce from bag in slow cooker, making sure it is about ½ to ⅔ full.

3. Cover and cook on LOW for 6 to 7 hours, adding scallions during the last 15 minutes of cooking.

Chicken and Stuffing

SERVINGS 4 to 6 portions **I COOK TIME** 4 hours

Marinate chicken with Italian seasoning mix.

Ingredients

1 ½ lbs. boneless, skinless chicken breasts

1 (6-oz.) box stuffing mix

½ c. sour cream

1 (10 ¾-oz.) can cream of chicken, cream of mushroom or cream of celery soup

Directions

1. Add chicken to slow cooker and top with dry stuffing mix. Combine sour cream and soup in a small mixing bowl and pour mixture over chicken.

2. Cover and cook on LOW for 4 hours.

3. Stir ingredients and serve.

BBQ Burgers

YIELD 6 portions **I COOK TIME** 7 to 9 hours

Garnish with mushrooms or mix them into your patties.

Ingredients

1   medium white onion, minced

2   lbs. ground beef

1   egg, lightly beaten

    Salt and pepper, to taste

2   c. BBQ sauce

Directions

1. Combine beef, onion and egg in a bowl and mix until well combined. Add salt and pepper.

2. Shape beef into 6 (¾-in.) patties, then stack in slow cooker. Add sauce.

3. Cover and cook on LOW for 7 to 9 hours.

Easy Eggplant Parmesan

YIELD 10 to 12 portions **|**
COOK TIME 5 to 6 hours on
HIGH or 8 hours on LOW

Ingredients

- 2 (16-oz.) jars marinara sauce
- 2 large eggplants, peeled and
     thinly sliced
-    Italian seasoned breadcrumbs
- ½–¾ c. grated Parmesan cheese
- 3 c. shredded mozzarella cheese

Directions

1. Add marinara, eggplant, bread crumbs, Parmesan, more marinara and mozzarella in greased slow cooker in 3 to 4 layers.

2. Cover and cook on HIGH for 5 to 6 hours or on LOW for 8 hours.

All the flavor of a classic parm with way fewer calories!

The Main Event

Cowboy Casserole

YIELD 4 to 6 portions |
COOK TIME 7 to 9 hours

Ingredients

1 ½ lbs. ground chuck

1 small yellow onion, chopped

6 medium red potatoes, sliced

1 (15-oz.) can red beans, drained

1 (10 ¾-oz.) can tomato soup

Salt, to taste

Pepper, to taste

Garlic, to taste, optional

Directions

1. Brown ground beef in skillet. Drain and remove.

2. Place onion, beef, potatoes and beans in slow cooker. Add soup, salt, pepper and garlic, if desired.

3. Cover and cook on LOW for 7 to 9 hours.

Cola Pork Roast

YIELD 6 portions I **COOK TIME** 4 to 5 hours on HIGH or 8 to 10 hours on LOW

There's no better way to top a roast than with gravy.

Ingredients

- 3 lbs. pork butt
- 1 (12-oz.) can cola
- 1 (10 ¾-oz.) can cream of mushroom soup
- 1 (2-oz.) envelope onion soup mix

Directions

1. Place roast in slow cooker.

2. Mix cola, mushroom soup and onion soup mix and pour over roast.

3. Cover and cook on HIGH for 4 to 5 hours or on LOW for 8 to 10 hours.

Sausage and Peppers

YIELD 5 portions I **COOK TIME** 3 to 4 hours on HIGH or 6 to 8 hours on LOW

Cooked pasta makes it a meal. Eat up!

Ingredients

- 1   medium yellow onion, sliced
- 3 ½   bell peppers, sliced
- 2 ½   lbs. mild Italian sausage
- 1   (28-oz.) can stewed tomatoes
- 1   (24-oz.) jar marinara sauce

Directions

1. Put onions and peppers in the bottom of slow cooker. Arrange sausage on top of vegetables. Pour the stewed tomatoes on top of the sausage, then the marinara sauce.

2. Cover and cook on HIGH for 3 to 4 hours or on LOW for 6 to 8 hours.

Sour Cream Salsa Chicken

YIELD 4 portions **I COOK TIME** 6 to 8 hours

Ingredients

- 2 lbs. boneless, skinless chicken breasts
- 1 (1-oz.) envelope taco seasoning mix
- 1 c. salsa
- ¼ c. sour cream

Directions

1. Add chicken, taco seasoning and salsa to slow cooker.

2. Cover and cook on LOW for 6 to 8 hours.

3. Shred chicken, remove from slow cooker and stir in sour cream.

Serve chicken in tortillas with desired toppings.

Beer Brats

YIELD 8 portions **| COOK TIME** 6 to 7 hours

Ingredients

2   T. olive oil

2   cloves garlic, chopped

8   bratwursts

1   (18-oz.) bottle beer

Directions

1. Heat oil and garlic in a large skillet over medium. Add bratwurst and brown each side. Use a fork to poke holes in the bratwursts and cook for 5 more minutes. Transfer brats to slow cooker. Add beer.

2. Cover and cook on LOW for 6 to 7 hours.

❯❯ Load Them Up

Serve bratwursts on lightly toasted buns with sauerkraut, onions, green and red bell peppers, pepperoncini rings, hot peppers, spicy mustard, ketchup or relish. Almost every combination makes for a delicious dog!

The Main Event

Bacon and BBQ Chicken Sandwiches

YIELD 6 to 8 portions **I COOK TIME** 3 to 4 hours on HIGH or 6 to 7 hours on LOW

Drizzle sandwiches with reserved sauce.

Ingredients

- 2 lbs. boneless, skinless chicken breasts
- 2 c. BBQ sauce
- 6-8 large buns
- 12-16 slices bacon, cooked and crumbled
- 2 c. shredded cheddar cheese

Directions

1. Add chicken breasts to greased or lined slow cooker. Pour in BBQ sauce.

2. Cover and cook on HIGH for 3 to 4 hours or on LOW for 6 to 7 hours.

3. Remove chicken and shred. Return meat to slow cooker and stir.

4. Preheat oven to 425 degrees F. Line a baking sheet with foil and add bottom buns. Top with a scoop of BBQ chicken, 2 slices worth of crumbled bacon and some cheese. Transfer pan to the oven and cook for 3 to 4 minutes.

5. Remove pan from oven, top sandwiches with remaining buns and serve.

Pork Chops and Gravy

YIELD 4 portions **I COOK TIME** 6 to 8 hours

Ingredients

- 4   bone-in or boneless pork chops
- 1   (2-oz.) envelope onion soup mix
- 1 ½   cups chicken broth
- 1   (10 ½-oz.) can cream of chicken soup
- 1   (1-oz.) envelope dry pork gravy mix

Directions

1. Place pork chops in slow cooker. Combine the remaining ingredients and pour the mixture over the pork chops.

2. Cover and cook on LOW for 6 to 8 hours.

For thicker gravy, stir in flour or heavy cream when cook time is almost finished.

Flavor-Packed
Cheese Ravioli

YIELD 4 portions **I COOK TIME** 6 hours 15 minutes

Ingredients

- 1 large carrot, sliced, optional
- 1 medium yellow onion, chopped, optional
- 2 cloves garlic, minced
- 2 (14-oz.) cans vegetable broth
- 2 (14-oz.) cans Italian-style diced tomatoes
- 1 (15-oz.) can cannellini beans, rinsed and drained
- ⅛ t. pepper
- 1 t. dried basil leaves, optional
- ½ c. grated Parmesan cheese, optional
- 1 (9-oz.) package cheese stuffed ravioli pasta

  Mozzarella cheese, optional

Serve pasta and veggies plain or with marinara sauce.

Directions

1. Combine carrots, onion, garlic, vegetable broth, tomatoes, cannellini beans and pepper in slow cooker. Top with basil and Parmesan, if desired.

2. Cover and cook on LOW for 6 hours.

3. Increase heat to HIGH and stir in ravioli. Cover and cook for 15 minutes until ravioli are tender, then serve with mozzarella, if desired.

Easy
Orange Chicken

Add orange slices to slow cooker during the last 30 minutes of cooking.

YIELD 4 to 5 portions **I COOK TIME** 3 hours 30 minutes

Ingredients

- 2 lbs. boneless, skinless chicken breasts
- ½ c. chicken broth
- ¾ c. orange marmalade
- ¾ c. BBQ sauce
- 2 T. soy sauce

Directions

1. Add chicken and broth to slow cooker.

2. Cover and cook on HIGH for 3 hours.

3. Drain broth from slow cooker. Combine orange marmalade, BBQ sauce and soy sauce until well mixed. Pour over chicken.

4. Cover and cook on HIGH for an additional 30 minutes.

The Main Event

Oktoberfest Kielbasa

YIELD 6 portions **I COOK TIME** 4 to 5 hours

If you aren't serving a large crowd, feel free to keep the sausages whole.

Ingredients

1 (32-oz.) jar sauerkraut

½ medium red cabbage, shredded

1-1½ lbs. beef kielbasa, cut into ½-in. pieces

Directions

1. Pour sauerkraut in slow cooker. Add cabbage and stir. Place kielbasa in slow cooker around the edges to form a ring. Use excess kielbasa to start a second ring inside the first.

2. Cover and cook on LOW for 4 to 5 hours.

Soda-Soaked Ribs

YIELD 6 to 8 portions |
COOK TIME 6 hours

Ingredients

3   lbs. ribs

1   (12-oz.) can cola

    Salt, to taste

    Pepper, to taste

2   c. BBQ sauce

1   medium white onion, chopped

Directions

1. Add ribs, soda, salt and pepper to slow cooker.

2. Cover and cook on HIGH for 5 hours.

3. Drain juices and add BBQ sauce and onions.

4. Cover and cook on HIGH for 1 hour.

The Main Event

Hawaiian BBQ Chicken

YIELD 4 to 6 portions **|**
COOK TIME 2 to 3 hours on HIGH
or 4 to 6 hours on LOW

Ingredients

- 2 lbs. boneless, skinless chicken breasts
- 2 c. Hawaiian-style BBQ sauce
- 1 (20-oz.) can pineapple chunks, drained
- 1 small yellow onion, diced
- 1 small green pepper, diced

Directions

1. Place all ingredients in slow cooker, making sure the chicken is well coated.

2. Cover and cook on HIGH for 2 to 3 hours or on LOW for 4 to 6 hours.

3. Shred chicken, return meat to slow cooker, stir and serve.

Crab Legs

YIELD 2 to 3 portions **I COOK TIME** 4 hours to 4 hours 30 minutes

Look thoroughly through crab chambers so you do not miss meat.

Ingredients

3 lbs. snow crab legs

½ c. unsalted butter, melted, plus more to serve

4 cloves garlic, minced

1 t. dill

Lemons, cut into wedges, to serve

Directions

1. Place crab legs in slow cooker and add just enough water to cover.

2. Combine butter, garlic and dill in a small bowl, then pour the mixture over the crab legs.

3. Cover and cook on HIGH for 4 hours (or 4 hours 30 minutes if using frozen legs).

4. Serve hot with butter and lemons.

Honey-Seared
Pork Tenderloin

YIELD 4 to 5 portions **I COOK TIME** 3 hours

Ingredients

1½–2 lbs. pork tenderloin

⅔ c. honey

4 T. soy sauce

2 T. packed brown sugar

3 T. sesame oil, optional

4 T. balsamic vinegar

Directions

1. Place tenderloin in slow cooker. Combine the remaining ingredients in a bowl, then pour sauce into slow cooker.

2. Cover and cook on LOW for 1 hour 30 minutes.

3. Flip tenderloin, cover and cook on LOW for 1 hour 30 minutes.

4. Let tenderloin sit for 10 minutes, slice, then serve.

≫ Serve It With Sauce

Combine 3 T. Dijon mustard, 5 T. honey and 2 T. rice wine vinegar to create a heavenly sauce to serve alongside your tenderloin. Whisk the mixture until smooth, then pour over slices of pork.

Lemon Pesto Salmon Fillet

YIELD 4 portions **I COOK TIME** 2 to 3 hours

Both homemade and store-bought pesto will work in this recipe.

Ingredients

- 1 lemon, cut in half
- ½ c. pesto sauce
- ½ t. salt
- ½ t. pepper
- 4 (6-oz.) salmon fillets

Directions

1. Slice ½ of the lemon into thin slices and reserve.

2. Squeeze juice from remaining ½ lemon into a small bowl. Blend with pesto, salt and pepper.

3. Whisk to combine.

4. Place the salmon in slow cooker, cover with pesto mixture and top with lemon juice.

5. Cover and cook on LOW for 2 to 3 hours.

Orange and Honey Tilapia

YIELD 4 portions **I COOK TIME** 2 hours to 2 hours 30 minutes

Ingredients

- 4 (6-oz.) tilapia fillets
- 2 T. balsamic vinegar
- 1 T. honey
- 1 T. Dijon mustard
- 1 (10-oz.) can mandarin oranges, drained
- Salt, to taste
- Pepper, to taste

Directions

1. Combine balsamic vinegar, honey and Dijon mustard in a small bowl.

2. Lay foil on your countertop and place the fish in the middle. Spread the sauce mixture over the top of each fillet. Add oranges. Fold over foil and crimp the edges to form a packet.

2. Transfer the foil packet into slow cooker and cover.

3. Cook on HIGH for 2 hours to 2 hours 30 minutes, or until fish flakes easily with a fork.

4. Remove fish from foil, add salt and pepper, then serve.

Apple-Glazed Pork Roast

YIELD 6 portions |
COOK TIME 10 to 12 hours

Ingredients

4   lbs. pork loin roast

     Salt, to taste

     Pepper, to taste

6   apples, cored and quartered

¼   c. apple juice

3   T. packed brown sugar

1   t. ground ginger

Directions

1. Rub roast with salt and pepper to season. Brown under broiler to remove excess fat; drain well.

2. Place apples in the bottom of slow cooker, followed by the pork. Combine apple juice, brown sugar and ginger. Spoon over roast.

3. Cover and cook on LOW for 10 to 12 hours.

Buffalo Chicken Wrap

YIELD 8 portions **I COOK TIME** 3 to 4 hours

Wrap your favorite veggies in with the chicken.

Ingredients

1 ½ lbs. boneless, skinless chicken breasts, cut into chunks

¾ c. buffalo sauce

¾ c. ranch dressing

Garlic salt, to taste

8 tortillas, to serve

Blue cheese dressing, to serve

Directions

1. Combine chicken, buffalo sauce and ranch dressing in slow cooker. Sprinkle with garlic salt, if desired.

2. Cover and cook on LOW for 3 to 4 hours.

3. Serve chicken in tortillas with blue cheese dressing, if desired.

The Main Event

Creamy
Chicken Tacos

It almost goes without saying, but the more cream cheese you use, the creamier tacos will be.

YIELD 8 portions **I COOK TIME** 3 to 4 hours on HIGH or 5 to 6 hours on LOW

Ingredients

1 ½ lbs. chicken breast

1 (15-oz.) jar salsa

1 (1-oz.) envelope taco seasoning

½–1 (8-oz.) package cream cheese

8 tortilla shells, to serve

Directions

1. Combine chicken, salsa, taco seasoning and cream cheese in slow cooker.

2. Cover and cook on HIGH for 3 to 4 hours or on LOW for 5 to 6 hours.

3. Remove chicken from slow cooker and shred. Return meat, stir and serve in tortilla shells.

Smoked Sausage, Green Beans and Potatoes

YIELD 4 portions **I COOK TIME** 4 to 6 hours

Ingredients

- 4 medium red potatoes, peeled and cubed
- ½ medium yellow onion, sliced
- 2 (14 ½-oz.) cans green beans, drained
- ½ t. pepper
- Salt, to taste
- 1 lb. kielbasa or smoked sausage, cut into bite-sized pieces

Directions

1. Combine all ingredients (except sausage) in slow cooker. Add water until ingredients are just covered.

2. Cover and cook on LOW for 4 to 6 hours, or until potatoes are tender. Add sausage 1 hour before cook time ends. Do not stir until ready to serve.

If you like your green beans to snap, use fresh beans and add them when you pour in the sausage.

Pineapple-Marinated Pork Chops

YIELD 6 portions **I** **COOK TIME** 6 to 8 hours

Ingredients

- 1 (20-oz.) can pineapple chunks
- ¼ c. packed brown sugar
- 2 t. soy sauce
- 6 pork chops

Directions

1. Mix pineapple, brown sugar and soy sauce in a plastic storage bag. Add pork chops, shake to coat and refrigerate for 8 hours.

2. Transfer to slow cooker.

3. Cover and cook on LOW for 6 to 8 hours.

Serve over pineapple mixture from slow cooker.

Frankfurters with Macaroni and Cheese

YIELD 8 portions **I** **COOK TIME** 3 to 4 hours

Ingredients

2 ⅔ c. macaroni

1 (12-oz.) can evaporated skim milk

1 c. skim milk

2 c. shredded cheddar cheese

8 hot dogs, diced

1 t. dried parsley flakes, optional

Directions

1. Combine all ingredients in slow cooker and mix well.

2. Cover and cook on LOW for 3 to 4 hours.

Combine 1 c. breadcrumbs, 2 T. melted butter and 1 c. shredded cheddar cheese to create an optional topping.

Simple
Chicken

YIELD 8 portions **I COOK TIME** 8 to 10 hours

Ingredients

1   whole chicken

     Salt, to taste

     Pepper, to taste

     Garlic powder, to taste

     Onion powder, to taste

     Paprika, to taste

1–2   T. water

Directions

1. Season chicken on all sides with salt, pepper, garlic powder, onion powder and paprika. Add water to slow cooker, followed by the seasoned chicken.

2. Cover and cook on LOW for 8 to 10 hours.

Broth Bonus

When you remove your chicken from the slow cooker, transfer the remaining liquid to a sealable container and refrigerate. Skim the fat from the top of the chicken broth, then use in future recipes. You can store it in your freezer!

Pepperoncini Venison Roast

When roast finishes cooking, meat should be tender and easy to shred.

YIELD 8 portions **I COOK TIME** 8 hours

Ingredients

- 4 lbs. venison rump roast, gristle and fat removed
- 2 (12-oz.) bottles beer
- 1 (16-oz.) jar pepperoncinis

Directions

1. Place venison in slow cooker. Add beer and pepperoncinis.
2. Cover and cook on LOW for 8 hours, or until meat is tender.

Glazed Pork Chops

YIELD 4 portions **I**
COOK TIME 8 hours

Ingredients

- 4 lbs. bone-in pork chops
- 1 (20-oz.) can pineapple chunks
- 2 c. apple juice
- 2 c. sweet BBQ sauce

Directions

1. Place all ingredients in slow cooker.

2. Cover and cook on LOW for 8 hours.

Slather chops with extra sauce just before serving.

The Main Event

Spaghetti Squash and Meatballs

YIELD 3 to 4 portions **I COOK TIME** 4 hours

Ingredients

- 1 large spaghetti squash
- 1 (16-oz.) jar marinara sauce
- 1 (16-oz.) package frozen meatballs, thawed
- Parmesan cheese, to garnish

Directions

1. Cut the spaghetti squash in half lengthwise. Scoop out the inside of the squash, including the seeds. Place squash halves side-by-side, cut side down, in slow cooker. Pour in ½ the marinara sauce. Add meatballs, followed by the remaining sauce over the meatballs.

2. Cover and cook on HIGH for 4 hours.

3. When finished, use a fork to shred the inside of the squash to make spaghetti. Top with sauce and meatballs. Garnish with Parmesan cheese and serve.

Chicken Cacciatore

YIELD 4 portions **I COOK TIME** 6 to 8 hours

Ingredients

1 lb. boneless, skinless chicken breasts, cut into chunks

1 (14 ½-oz.) can diced tomatoes

1 medium yellow onion, diced

1 large red pepper, chopped

1 T. Italian herbs

Pepper, to taste

2 cloves garlic, minced, optional

Directions

1. Combine all ingredients in slow cooker, making sure that chicken is well coated.

2. Cover and cook on LOW for 6 to 8 hours.

Serve over the pasta of your choice with a side of garlic bread for an unbeatable Italian cuisine.

BBQ Pulled Pork

YIELD 8 portions **I COOK TIME** 4 to 6 hours on HIGH or 8 to 10 hours on LOW

Ingredients

3–6 lbs. pork shoulder butt

1 medium yellow onion, quartered

1 (14-oz.) can beef broth

1 (16-oz.) bottle BBQ sauce

Directions

1. Place pork in slow cooker. Top with onions and broth.

2. Cover and cook on HIGH for 4 to 6 hours or on LOW for 8 to 10 hours.

3. Remove pork and onions. Shred the pork and cut onions into smaller chunks. Discard any fat, bone, gristle or broth. Return meat and onions to slow cooker. Add BBQ, stir and serve.

Pickles and fries make perfect companions.

Simple Sweets

Craving a little something extra without the extra work?
Look no further than the pages that follow.

Rice Krispies Treats

YIELD 12 portions **I COOK TIME** 1 hour

Ingredients

- 3 T. butter, cut into cubes
- 4 c. miniature marshmallows
- 2 (24-oz.) boxes crisped rice cereal

Directions

1. Add butter to slow cooker, followed by ½ the marshmallows, ½ the cereal, the remaining marshmallows and the remaining cereal.

2. Cover and cook on HIGH for 1 hour.

3. Stir well to combine ingredients. Transfer mixture to a greased 9- by 11-in. pan. Allow mixture to cool, cut into squares and serve.

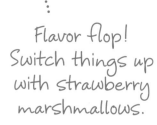

Flavor flop! Switch things up with strawberry marshmallows.

Simple Sweets

Very Cherry
Chocolate Cake

YIELD 12 portions **I COOK TIME** 3 hours

Ingredients

1 (21-oz.) can cherry pie filling

1 (18-oz.) box chocolate
   cake mix

½ c. butter

1 t. pure almond extract

   Whipped cream, to garnish

   Maraschino cherries, to garnish

Directions

1. Place pie filling in slow cooker.
Combine dry cake mix with butter
and almond extract and sprinkle
over filling.

2. Cover and cook on LOW for
3 hours.

3. Serve garnished with whipped
cream and maraschino cherries.

⧽⧽ A Piece of Cake

Altering this recipe to match your
diners' tastes is as easy as pie. As long as
ingredient quantities remain unchanged,
you can sub a different type of pie filling,
cake mix or extract without changing the
directions or the cook time.

Apple Caramel Pie

YIELD 8 portions **I COOK TIME** 3 hours

Optional addition: fresh apple slices. yum!

Ingredients

- 2   refrigerated pie crust doughs
- 2   (22-oz.) cans apple pie filling
- 1   t. ground cinnamon
- 12 caramels

Directions

1. Press 1 crust into ½ of the bottom of slow cooker and about 1 in. or so up the side. Add the second crust to the other side of slow cooker, overlapping in the center by about ¼ in. Press seams flat where the crusts meet.

2. Cover and cook on HIGH for 1 hour 30 minutes.

3. Combine apple pie filling, cinnamon and caramel pieces, then pour into slow cooker.

4. Cover and cook on LOW for 1 hour 30 minutes.

Pumpkin Angel Food Cake with Caramel Sauce

YIELD 8 portions **I COOK TIME** 4 hours

Ingredients

- 1 (16-oz.) box angel food cake mix
- 1 c. pure pumpkin
- 1 ½ t. pumpkin pie spice
- 1 t. pure vanilla extract
- 1 (14-oz.) can sweetened condensed milk

Directions

1. Preheat slow cooker on HIGH and prepare cake mix according to package directions in a bowl.

2. In a separate bowl, combine pumpkin, pie spice and vanilla. Combine mixture with cake mix.

3. Place unopened, clean paperless sweetened condensed milk can in the center of slow cooker. Pour cake mix into slow cooker around the can.

4. Cover and cook on HIGH for 2 hours.

5. After 2 hours, carefully remove sweetened condensed milk can and gently flip cake out onto a baking rack to cool.

6. Return can and 2 cups hot water to the slow cooker and continue to cook on HIGH for 2 hours while the cake cools.

7. Remove can and allow to cool. Carefully open to reveal caramel. Drizzle caramel over cake and serve.

Simple Sweets

Cherry Delight

YIELD 10 to 12 portions **I COOK TIME** 2 hours on HIGH or 4 hours on LOW

Ingredients

1 (21-oz.) can cherry pie filling

1 (15 ¼-oz.) box yellow cake mix

½ c. butter, melted

⅓ c. walnuts, optional

Directions

1. Place cherry pie filling in greased slow cooker.

2. Combine cake mix and butter, then sprinkle mixture over filling. Top with walnuts, if desired.

3. Cover and cook on HIGH for 2 hours or on LOW for 4 hours.

Feel free to add some fresh cherries, too.

Simple Sweets

Rocky Road Candy

YIELD 12 portions **I COOK TIME** 1 hour

Ingredients

1 (12-oz.) bag semisweet chocolate chips

2 c. miniature marshmallows

½ c. slivered almonds

Directions

1. Add chocolate to slow cooker.

2. Cover and cook on LOW for 1 hour, stirring occasionally.

3. Once chocolate is melted, stir in marshmallows and turn off slow cooker. Scoop candy onto a parchment-lined baking sheet immediately.

4. Top with slivered almonds, let sit for 10 minutes, then serve.

To contain the crunch, mix the almonds into the chocolate and miniature marshmallows.

Cinnamon
Apple Cobbler

YIELD 6 portions **I COOK TIME** 4 hours

Ingredients

- 1 (21-oz.) can apple pie filling
- 5–7 medium Granny Smith apples, peeled, cored and chopped
- 1 T. ground cinnamon
- 1 (15 ¼-oz.) box yellow cake mix
- ½ c. butter, melted

Directions

1. Combine pie filling, apples and cinnamon in the bottom of the slow cooker. Stir.

2. Top with cake mix, then drizzle with melted butter. Do not stir.

3. Cover and cook on HIGH for 4 hours.

» Top Notch Topper

To create an unbeatable crumble topping, combine 1 c. flour, ½ c. sugar, ¼ c. packed brown sugar, 2 t. ground cinnamon, ½ t. salt and 6 T. cold butter in a bowl. Pour mixture into the slow cooker when 1 hour of cook time remains.

Simple Sweets

Monkey Bread

YIELD 12 portions **I COOK TIME** 2 to 3 hours

Mix 1 c. powdered sugar and a couple T. of milk to create a glaze. Drizzle over monkey bread and enjoy.

Ingredients

- 1 c. butter, melted
- ½ c. sugar
- ½ c. packed dark brown sugar
- 4 t. ground cinnamon
- 1 (16.3-oz.) cylinder biscuits, quartered
- ½ c. chopped pecans, optional

Directions

1. Insert a greased liner into slow cooker.

2. Put melted butter in one bowl and combine sugars and cinnamon in another. Dip biscuits into butter, then roll in cinnamon sugar.

3. Layer biscuits snuggly into slow cooker. Add pecans, if using.

4. Place paper towel over the top of slow cooker.

5. Cover and cook on LOW for 2 to 3 hours.

6. When biscuits are done, remove liner and transfer to a plate. Remove bread from liner by rolling liner down the sides of plate. Slide bread off with a large spatula and serve.

Butterscotch Rum Dip

YIELD 8 to 10 portions **I COOK TIME** 45 to 50 minutes

Ingredients

2 (11-oz.) packages butterscotch chips

1 (5-oz.) can evaporated milk

⅔ c. chopped pecans, optional

1 T. rum

1 T. pure vanilla extract

Directions

1. Combine butterscotch and evaporated milk in slow cooker.

2. Cover and cook on LOW for 45 to 50 minutes, or until the chips are soft.

3. Stir until smooth, then add rum, vanilla and pecans, if using. Mix until well combined and serve.

If desired, you can sub pure rum extract for alcohol.

Simple Sweets

Chocolate Nut Clusters

YIELD 12 to 16 portions **I** **COOK TIME** 2 hours

Ingredients

- 2 lbs. vanilla almond bark
- 1 (4-oz.) German chocolate baking bar
- 1 (12-oz.) bag semisweet chocolate chips
- 3 c. dry roasted peanuts

Directions

1. Combine all ingredients in slow cooker.

2. Cover and cook on HIGH for 1 hour. Do not stir.

3. Reduce heat to LOW, cover and cook for 1 hour, stirring about every 15 minutes.

4. Drop spoonfuls of candy onto waxed paper, cool and serve.

Accounting for allergies is no problem. Pretzel pieces work great in place of nuts.

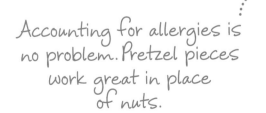

Triple
Chocolate Pecan Delight

YIELD 36 portions **I COOK TIME** 2 hours

Ingredients

- 3 c. pecans, coarsely chopped
- 2 lbs. vanilla almond bark, broken into pieces
- 1 (4-oz.) sweetened chocolate baking bar, broken into pieces
- 1 (12-oz.) bag semisweet chocolate chips

Directions

1. Toast pecans in a heavy skillet over medium heat for 1 to 2 minutes, or until pecans are lightly browned, stirring frequently.

2. Place all ingredients in slow cooker.

3. Cover and cook on HIGH for 1 hour. Do not stir.

4. Reduce heat to LOW, cover and cook for 1 hour, stirring about every 15 minutes.

5. Drop spoonfuls of candy onto waxed paper, let cool and serve.

Blueberry Dump Cake

YIELD 4 to 6 portions **I COOK TIME** 2 to 3 hours

Any kind of pie filling can be substituted into this recipe.

Ingredients

1   (21-oz.) can blueberry pie filling

1   (15 ¼-oz.) box yellow cake mix

½   c. butter, softened

Directions

1. Pour pie filling into the bottom of slow cooker.

2. Pour cake mix into a medium-sized bowl. Add butter and combine with clean hands. Carefully sprinkle on top of the pie filling.

3. Cover and cook on HIGH for 2 to 3 hours.

Simple Sweets

Classic
Tapioca Pudding

YIELD 8 portions **I COOK TIME** 3 hours on HIGH or 6 hours on LOW

Ingredients

- 2 eggs, lightly beaten
- 4 c. milk
- ⅔ c. sugar
- 2 t. pure vanilla extract
- ½ c. small pearl tapioca

Directions

1. Beat eggs with milk, sugar, vanilla and tapioca.

2. Cover and cook on HIGH for 3 hours or on LOW for 6 hours, stirring often.

3. Serve warm.

⫸ Plastic Placement

When you store your leftovers or chill your dessert to serve it cold, make sure that you cover it with plastic wrap, pressing on the surface of the pudding to keep it from drying out or developing a film.

Simple Sweets

Mixed Berry Crumble

YIELD 8 portions **I COOK TIME** 2 to 4 hours

Ingredients

- 1 (12-oz.) package frozen mixed berries
- ½ c. dried cranberries
- ⅓ c. cranberry juice cocktail
- ¼ c. minute quick-cooking tapioca
- 1 c. sugar
- ½ t. ground cinnamon, optional
- 1 c. baking mix, optional
- ¾ c. kashi cereal, optional
- 5 almond biscotti cookies, crushed, optional
- 2 T. butter, melted, optional

Directions

1. Add berries, dried cranberries, juice, tapioca, cinnamon and sugar to slow cooker.

2. Cover and cook on HIGH for 2 to 4 hours, or until fruit is tender.

3. For an optional crumble topping, preheat oven to 350 degrees F. Line a baking sheet with aluminum foil. Combine all optional ingredients in a bowl, then spread mixture on prepared sheet and bake for 12 to 18 minutes, or until crisp and golden. Serve over berry mixture.

Serve crumble à la mode or topped with whipped cream.

Caramel Rum Fondue

YIELD 8 portions **I** **COOK TIME** 2 hours

Ingredients

1   (14-oz.) package caramels

⅔ c. heavy cream or whipping cream

½ c. miniature marshmallows

2–3 t. rum

Directions

1. Combine caramels and cream in slow cooker.

2. Cover and cook on LOW for about 1 hour 30 minutes, or until caramels have melted.

3. Stir in marshmallows and rum until well blended.

4. Cover and cook on LOW for 30 minutes.

Drizzle onto your ice cream sundaes!

Simple Sweets

Chocolate Buckeye Candy

YIELD 10 portions **I COOK TIME** 30 minutes

Ingredients

½ c. peanut butter

⅓ c. butter

⅛ t. pure vanilla extract

2 c. powdered sugar

1 ⅓ c. semisweet chocolate chips

Directions

1. In a large bowl, mix peanut butter, butter, vanilla and powdered sugar.

2. Roll dough into 1-in. balls and place on a waxed paper-lined plate or cookie sheet. Chill in freezer until firm, about 30 minutes.

3. While dough is chilling, pour chocolate chips into slow cooker.

4. Cover and cook on HIGH for about 30 minutes, or until chocolate is melted. After dough is firm, dip balls into chocolate and coat entirely, except for the very top.

5. Return to cookie sheets and refrigerate until serving.

Chocolate Tapioca Pudding

YIELD 8 portions **I COOK TIME** 2 hours 30 minutes to 4 hours

Top pudding with your choice of fresh fruit.

Ingredients

8 c. milk

1 c. sugar

1 c. small pearl tapioca

3 eggs

1 T. unsweetened cocoa powder

1 t. pure almond extract, optional

Directions

1. Combine milk, sugar and tapioca in slow cooker and stir well to mix.

2. Cover and cook on HIGH for 2 to 3 hours.

3. Whisk together eggs, cocoa powder and almond extract, if desired, in a large bowl. Transfer ½ c. of slow cooker mixture to the bowl, whisking constantly. Add another ½ c. of mixture, whisking constantly, followed by another ½ c. Pour the egg mixture into slow cooker and stir thoroughly until combined.

4. Cover and cook on HIGH for 30 minutes to 1 hour, or until the tapioca swells and thickens.

5. Turn off slow cooker and remove lid. Let stand for 30 minutes.

6. Transfer pudding from slow cooker to a large bowl. Cover tapioca directly with plastic wrap and chill. Serve cold.

Simple Sweets

Glazed
Apple Pie Bread Pudding

YIELD 6 portions **I COOK TIME** 6 hours

Ingredients

- 12 slices bread, torn into pieces
- 3 medium apples, cored, peeled and chopped
- 1 c. apple juice
- ½ c. lemon-lime soda
- ½ c. sugar
- 1 ½ t. apple pie spice, optional

Directions

1. Combine bread and apples in greased slow cooker. Combine remaining ingredients and drizzle evenly over bread. Stir lightly.

2. Cover and cook on LOW for 6 hours.

3. Stir, then serve.

⟩⟩ Great Glaze

Nothing completes this tasty bread pudding like a homemade vanilla glaze. Combine 1 c. powdered sugar, 1 ½ T. milk and ¼ t. pure vanilla extract until well mixed. Pour glaze over individual servings of pudding.

Sweet and Salty
Fudge

YIELDS 36 pieces **I** **COOK TIME** 1 hour 30 minutes

Ingredients

- 1 ½ lbs. chocolate almond bark, broken into pieces
- 1 (4-oz.) unsweetened chocolate baking bar
- 2 c. salted nuts
- 2 c. miniature marshmallows, optional
- 1 (7-oz.) bag pretzels, crushed, optional

Directions

1. Add chocolate to slow cooker.

2. Cover and cook on LOW for 1 hour 30 minutes, or until mixture is smooth.

3. Unplug slow cooker, add nuts, pretzels and marshmallows, if desired, then stir.

4. Pour mixture into a greased 9- by 13-inch pan. Cool, cut into squares and serve.

If desired, garnish with sea salt.

Simple Sweets

Chocolate Marshmallow Lollipops

YIELDS 10 lollipops **I COOK TIME** 30 minutes

Roll some lollipops in candy for extra flair.

Ingredients

- 1 package chocolate candiquik
- 10 large marshmallows
- 10 lollipop sticks
-   Sprinkles, to garnish

Directions

1. Place chocolate in slow cooker.

2. Cover and cook on HIGH for 30 minutes, or until chocolate is melted, stirring as needed.

3. Reduce heat to LOW as soon as chocolate is melted.

4. Place marshmallows on lollipop sticks and dip into melted chocolate. Coat in sprinkles and stick lollipops, marshmallow side up, in a short glass or piece of styrofoam until chocolate sets.

Almond Bark

YIELD 10 portions **|**
COOK TIME 2 hours

Ingredients

- 1 c. whole unsalted almonds
- 1–1 ½ c. flaked coconut
- 1 (12-oz.) bag dark chocolate chips, 72% cacao or better
- 1 t. sea salt

Directions

1. Place a liner in slow cooker. Place almonds in slow cooker. Sprinkle in coconut and chocolate.

2. Cover and cook on LOW for 2 hours. Do not stir or remove lid.

3. Turn off slow cooker and uncover. Let cool in uncovered slow cooker for 3 to 4 hours, or until bark has set. Sprinkle top with sea salt.

4. Remove liner or parchment from crock carefully and place in fridge for 4 hours, or until firm. Remove from liner, cut and serve.

Simple Sweets

Black Forest Cake

YIELD 10 portions **I COOK TIME** 3 hours

Ingredients

- ½ c. butter, melted
- 1 (8-oz.) can crushed pineapple, drained and juice reserved
- 1 (21-oz.) can cherry pie filling
- 1 (15 ½-oz.) box chocolate cake mix

Directions

1. Combine melted butter and reserved pineapple juice in a small bowl. Set mixture aside.

2. Spread crushed pineapple in slow cooker, then top with cherry pie filling, followed by cake mix. Pour butter mixture over the dry cake mix.

3. Cover and cook on LOW for 3 hours.

Garnish with chocolate syrup, fresh cherries and whipped cream.

Caramel Pie

YIELD 6 to 8 portions **I COOK TIME** 3 to 4 hours

Ingredients

- 2 (14-oz.) cans sweetened condensed milk
- 1 (9-in.) graham cracker pie crust or baked pie crust
- 1 (8-oz.) container whipped topping

Directions

1. Pour condensed milk into slow cooker.

2. Cover and cook on LOW for 3 to 4 hours, or until milk is the color of peanut butter, whisking once or twice per hour.

3. Pour milk into crust and cool in the refrigerator.

4. Spread whipped topping over pie.

5. Cover and chill until ready to serve.

Healthier
Cinnamon Fudge

YIELD 20 portions **I COOK TIME** 2 hours

For a little extra sweetness, add a touch of brown sugar.

Ingredients

2 ½ c. dark chocolate chips

¼ c. coconut milk

¼ c. raw honey

1 dash sea salt, plus more to garnish

1 t. pure vanilla extract

1 t. ground cinnamon

Directions

1. Add chocolate, coconut milk, honey and sea salt to greased slow cooker. Stir to combine.

2. Cover and cook on LOW for 2 hours. Do not stir or lift lid.

3. Turn slow cooker off and uncover. Add vanilla and cinnamon. Stir to combine. Cool in uncovered slow cooker for 3 to 4 hours, or until fudge reaches room temperature.

4. Stir fudge for several minutes until sheen from the top is gone. Pour the fudge into greased 1-qt. glass dish. Cover and refrigerate for 4 hours, or until firm.

5. Garnish with sea salt, if desired, cut and serve.

Simple Sweets

Creamy
Pumpkin
Cranberry Custard

YIELD 8 portions **I** **COOK TIME** 4 hours

Ingredients

1   (30-oz.) can pure pumpkin

1   (12-oz.) can evaporated milk

1   c. dried cranberries

4   eggs, beaten

Directions

1. Combine all ingredients in slow cooker.

2. Cover and cook on HIGH for 4 hours.

⟫ That's a Snap!

Crush ginger snap cookies in a zip-top bag and stir into custard when cook time is nearly finished, if desired. The fall flavors complement each other beautifully. Garnish with whipped cream and dried cranberries, then serve.

Simple Sweets

Conversion Guide

Volume

¼ teaspoon = 1 mL

½ teaspoon = 2 mL

1 teaspoon = 5 mL

1 tablespoon = 15 mL

¼ cup = 50mL

⅓ cup = 75 mL

½ cup = 125 mL

⅔ cup = 150 mL

¾ cup = 175 mL

1 cup = 250 mL

1 quart = 1 liter

Weight

1 ounce = 30 grams

2 ounces = 55 grams

3 ounces = 85 grams

4 ounces (¼ pound) = 115 grams

8 ounces (½ pound) = 225 grams

16 ounces (1 pound) = 455 grams

2 pounds = 910 grams

Temperatures

32° Fahrenheit = 0° Celsius

212°F = 100°C

250°F = 120°C

275°F =140°C

300°F = 150°C

325°F = 160°C

350°F = 180°C

375°F = 190°C

400°F = 200°C

425°F = 220°C

450°F = 230°C

475°F = 240°C

500°F = 260°C

Length

⅛ inch = 3 mm

¼ inch = 6 mm

½ inch = 13 mm

¾ inch = 19 mm

1 inch = 2 ½ cm

2 inches = 5 cm

Media Lab Books
For inquiries, call 646-838-6637

Copyright 2015 Topix Media Lab

Published by Topix Media Lab
14 Wall Street, Suite 4B
New York, NY 10005

Printed in the USA

ISBN-10: 1-942556-18-7
ISBN-13: 978-1-942556-18-3

Indexing by R studio T, NYC

Special Thanks: Marsha Bare, Rachel Garmers

ON THE COVER: Sporrer/Skowronek/StockFood. Photography by Jenn Bare, iStock, Shutterstock, Thinkstock except: Darryl Brooks/FOTOLIA: 87; JJAVA/FOTOLIA: 116, 226; Sean Locke/Stocksy: 112; Sporrer/Skowronek/StockFood: 128.

Index

Hawaiian BBQ Chicken 186